CLOSING TIME AT
THE ROYAL OAK

Other books by John Lucas of related interest

The Good That We Do: The Life of a Junior School Teacher 1880–1940. (2000)

92 Acharnon Street: a Year in Athens. Winner of the 2008 Dolmen Award for Travel Writing

Next Year Will Be Better: A Memoir of England in the 1950s. A 2011 Book of the Year in the *Guardian* and *Times Literary Supplement.*

A Brief History of Whistling. With Allan Chatburn. 2013 (reprinted 2021)

The Awkward Squad: Rebels in English Cricket. Shortlisted for the Cricket Writers Book of the Year Awar, 2015 (reprinted 2016)

CLOSING TIME AT THE ROYAL OAK

JOHN LUCAS

Shoestring Press

Printed by imprintdigital
Upton Pyne, Exeter
www.digital.imprint.co.uk

Typesetting and cover design by The Book Typesetters
us@thebooktypesetters.com
07422 598 168
www.thebooktypesetters.com

Published by Shoestring Press
19 Devonshire Avenue, Beeston, Nottingham, NG9 1BS
0115 925 1827
www.shoestringpress.co.uk

First published 2021
© Copyright: John Lucas
© Cover photograph: Pauline Lucas

ISBN 978-1-912524-92-1

Acknowledgements

To Rachel and Nigel Lucas for exemplary editorial work, and, as always, to my beloved designers and typesetters, Rachael and Nathanael Ravenlock, now and henceforth to be known as The Book Typesetters, and to me as simply the best in the land.

A special thanks to Sue Wild, without whose technical assistance this book could not have been presented to the public.

To the memory of The Royal Oak, Beeston

Contents

Introduction

In the summer of nineteen sixty-four I was appointed to a lectureship in the English department of Nottingham University. Pauline and I, together with our two-year-old son, Ben, packed up the contents of our tumbledown flat in Reading – it didn't take long – and moved to a small semi-detached house in a featureless Nottingham suburb where a few months later, on a cold, foggy December evening, our daughter Emma was born. For three further years we continued to live in what in a poem I called prim, dull Wollaton. Then, a blessed break. In nineteen sixty-seven I was awarded a Fulbright Scholarship and, with it, a visiting professorship at the University of Maryland and, for the summer of nineteen sixty-eight, Indiana.

That was a wondrous year, and by the time it came to an end we'd promised ourselves that as soon as we got back to Nottingham we'd set about finding a different, larger house for our children to grow up in. Property in and around the city at the end of the nineteen-sixties was easy and cheap to come by. The house we settled on, tall, three-storey, semi-detached, was in Beeston, itself a small town – to all intents and purposes a suburb – scarcely a mile from the University campus. The asking price being no more than twice my annual salary, arranging a mortgage was a doddle, and in January nineteen sixty-nine, and with the help of a number of my students – bribed with offers of food and beer – we moved into the house where we've lived ever since.

A former Methodist manse, our new home was well-nigh perfect for us. The only hitch came when the Methodist church, before it would agree to the sale, insisted I sign a form promising not to sell spiritous liquor on the premises. I signed and the house was ours; and though for a while we received regular late night calls from people begging me to come quickly, as 'mester's on't brink,' these gradually petered out, as did the various pamphlets advertising patent remedies for ridding pews and roof beams of woodworm which from time to time flopped through our letter box.

Within a month of our moving in, Pauline, who had been for an exploratory walk round Beeston, returned with the news that, among various food shops which looked well worth trying out, she had noticed a pub up a side street, no more than a lane off the High Street, and directly across from a small lace factory. Villa Street, the lane's name was, and as for the pub, 'It's called the Royal Oak,' she said. 'It's your sort of pub.'

And so that evening, after the children had been tucked up in their beds, I put on my coat, left our house, and, following Pauline's directions, strolled round to Villa Street.

And there it was. The Royal Oak. It was no larger than a moderate-sized detached house or, of course, villa, which perhaps it had once been, and its two bay windows were separated by a central front door that opened straight off the street. It *was* my sort of pub, and for some twenty years it proved to be a place I would grow to cherish, even love. Hence, the following pages.

Part One: Chris and Margaret

1: The Singer

Chris glanced up at the clock above the bar. Nine-thirty. 'Any moment now,' he said, pulling a pint of mixed, which he placed on the bar. 'Tin hats at the ready, ladies and gents.'

As he spoke the street door swung open and into the tiled passage marched the man we all knew as Sheffield Tommy. He was dressed in his usual Friday evening outfit. Out-at-elbow Harris tweed sports jacket, chocolate-brown cords, white shirt with regimental tie and, above his battered face, which beamed with good will, a pork-pie hat worn at a modest but determined angle.

'Evenin' all,' he said as he arrived at the bar counter. He picked up the full glass Chris pushed across to him, raised it to eye level, made a show of inspecting it, lowered it to his lips, drank half the contents in one prolonged swallow, and returned the glass to the bar counter before saying 'As good as ever, landlord.' An appreciative nod. 'As I have often remarked, a man would go a long day's route march before tasting a finer beer than this one.'

'I bet you say that to all the publicans you meet.'

'I shall ignore those words,' Tommy said. He lifted his hat and removed a packet of ten Senior Service from where it perched on his virtually bald head. Opening the packet, he stared with some deliberation at its contents before selecting a cigarette, said, 'Would one of you gentlemen be so good,' and as he put the cigarette to his lips Harold sprang his lighter.

Sheffield Tommy inhaled, bowed his thanks, slowly blew some smoke toward the ceiling and, glancing about him, announced, 'All present and correct, I see.'

The unvarying routine. I'd been coming to the Oak for two years now and I knew what to expect of Tommy's Friday night performances. Five minutes to finish his drink, order and pay for another, and then the singing would begin. And at that moment the passage would empty and those gathered round the pumps would either take their drinks into the room on the left – the thronged, smoke-filled Public Bar where tonight the Ladies' Darts Team had a rare (and postponed) home fixture – or, if they fancied a quieter atmosphere, a few of them would migrate to the Saloon Bar on the right.

That left three of us standing in the passage, prepared to listen.

'Right, then, Mario Lanza,' Chris told him, 'you can have one song. What's it going to be? Not "Cara Mia Mine", by any chance?'

'Landlord, you anticipate my very thought. "Cara Mia Mine" it is.'

Tommy sang well, no doubt about it. His voice, a light tenor, was sure of pitch, full-toned, strong.

As the last note faded away he turned smiling to me and I nodded approval.

Tommy thanked me. Then, '"Thomas," Churchill said to me, when he was visiting the troops in Egypt, "Thomas, if the British Army was made up of men with your spirit, we'd have those Nazi bastards on the run soon enough."'

He downed his pint. 'I may have mentioned that before,' he said.

'You have, Tommy, you have,' Chris said, re-filling the glass the singer had pushed across the counter. 'And as I think I replied, your bloody voice would have been quite enough to put the enemy to flight without any need of tanks.'

'Jealousy surrounds me,' Tommy said to the ceiling. 'I bear no ill will. I may sing again.'

'Try and I'll get Harold and John here to put you out on your arse.'

There was no harm in Sheffield Tommy. A dishwasher at the university's student canteen, he was paid his week's wages on a Friday, on which morning and in anticipation of the evening's pleasure, he invariably marched to work dressed for his night out. His day's work being at an end by eight o'clock that evening, he promptly hung up his apron, donned jacket and hat, left the premises, and was into The Prince of Wales by ten past, where spies reported he drank two pints before heading further up to the High Street and The Greyhound for two more two pints, after which he dropped in on The Malt Shovel for a quick one before heading further up the High Street in order to make a right turn onto Villa Street and so to The Royal Oak, where he would arrive without fail at what he called the witching hour of nine-thirty. And an hour later, as Chris rang his hand bell before draping towels over the beer pumps, Tommy, singing as he went, left with all the others to make for home, which in his case was a one room bed-sitter, so rumour had it, at Hyson Green, on the other side of the city.

Why then choose to do his drinking here, in Beeston? There were after all plenty of good pubs up at Hyson Green, beside the many that were all around in that part of the city. From Beeston to the Green was a tidy step whichever route you took. The likeliest was out of Villa Street, down Wollaton Road, follow Derby Road up to Canning Circus, along Alfreton Road to join Gregory Boulevard, then up to the Green. Two miles at least, though others reckoned nearer three.

So, 'Why us?' Chris had once apparently asked. 'What have *we* done to deserve you, Tommy?'

Tommy, it was reported, treated the question seriously. 'I find the hostelries here more conducive to elegant conversation, besides which their décor is better suited to a man of my taste. Furthermore, the nearest is a mere ten minutes from my place of work. And besides,' – here, he drew himself up to his full height of five foot three – 'I am a Shipstone's man.'

Ah, Shipstone's. Beeston's pubs were mostly owned by Shippo's, one of three breweries which more or less divided the city between them. Home Ales, with its handsome art deco brewery on the far edge of Nottingham, owned a good many of the pubs in the city centre, although Shipstone, founded earlier and still using Shire horses to haul their barrel-loaded drays, was, I always felt, preferred by working class drinkers. For one thing its Public Bars encouraged a wide variety of board games – dominoes, shove ha'penny, table quoits, cribbage – and covered skittle alleys up the yard, skittles being a feature of most Shippo pubs. Few Home Ale pubs had such alleys, so at least the rumour ran. And as for those who drank in pubs owned by the Mansfield Brewery, they were viewed with a mixture of pity and incomprehension. It wasn't done to put in a good word for Mansfield ales, not in general company.

'I am a Shipstone's man.' Some wag had anagrammatised the brewery's name to 'Honest Piss,' but that didn't lessen the devotion of those who swore by its beer, especially the 'mixed' – half bitter, half mild, only available in pints, and, according to all, an ideal blend of malt and hops. Some drinkers muttered about the bitter on its own causing 'bladder rot', but most of us simply preferred the taste of mixed. And mixed was Tommy's tipple. He maintained it kept his throat in perfect condition. 'Three pints of that, and I could sing all night long.'

Did he have any friends? Looking back, trying in the light of what happened to recall as much as possible about him, I don't think he did. In the dim strip lighting of the pub's passage I'd sometimes glance at that battered face, the flattened nose I thought might have come from a bruising encounter with some toper bigger and heavier than him, but which Harold among others reckoned to be the evidence of a dose of the clap, and I'd see, or thought I could see in those watery blue eyes, a kind of desperate loneliness; but that might have been my own, sentimental assumption. Certainly whenever Tommy was asked how he was, how he fared, the answer was always the same. 'Most contentful, kind sir. The enemy is out of sight.'

It was almost a speech, a public utterance, an affirmation. And at the end of each Friday evening Tommy would leave the pub, shoulders back, head erect, and as he disappeared into the night you'd hear his voice dwindling along the high street as he sang – always – 'Pack Up Your Troubles in Your Old Kit Bag, and Smile, Smile, Smi…i…le,' the last word drawn out and made into a swelling diapason, though whether he sang for the entirety of his homeward trek I doubt. By the time Tommy was safe indoors and bedded down for the night the effect of the evening's beer, seven or eight pints of it, would surely have begun to wear off.

2: Helping Harold

Next morning, after an early breakfast, I walked round to Harold's house. The route took me past The Royal Oak, where I stopped for a quick chat with Chris, who was sweeping up the detritus from the previous evening.

'Where you off to, then?' he asked. 'I'm not open for another two hours.'

'Being taken for a ride by Harold,' I said. 'We arranged it last night. He wants me to go with him while he looks over some bits and pieces of furniture. A farm out toward Grantham is turning itself into a guest house, so he says, and he's put in a bid for the contents. Not all of them, of course. It's the kitchen-ware he's interested in. He reckons there'll be plenty of buyers for that. '

'Old totters never die,' Chris said. 'You do this often?'

I shook my head. 'I've helped him once or twice before. I quite enjoy the experience and Harold's good company.'

A dustbin stood in the pub doorway and Chris, looking up from his task of emptying into it a shovelful of crumpled crisp packets and butt-ends, said, 'Don't suppose he'd want any of this, do you? Bloody oiks.'

He leaned on his broom. 'I reckon some of them take pleasure in carrying the stuff outside and chucking it into the road. Doesn't matter how many times I ask them not to, they must think they haven't had a good night without making more work for me than I deserve.'

Chris's especial ire was directed at someone we called Big Bob. Bob always made a great show of wanting his table kept clean. Night after night he'd be the first through the Oak's street door, from where he'd march into the Saloon Bar, or as he preferred to call it, 'The Lounge', shrug himself out of the heavy check overcoat he wore whatever the weather, hang it behind the door, take a packet of twenty Player's from his jacket pocket, undo the cellophane wrap, open the packet, remove the silver paper foil, scrumple cellophane and foil in his large fist, drop the tangled mess on the floor, take his seat – Bob's Seat – at the small round wooden-topped table – Bob's Table – beside the Lounge fireplace, inspect the ashtray to ensure it was clean as well as empty, and then, as he lit his first cigarette, wait for Chris to bring him a glass, which he would also inspect for cleanliness, and a large bottle of brown ale, one of six he would drink during the course of an evening. As he was a chain smoker, he required Chris to reappear at regular intervals, not always when another bottle was due, to empty his ashtray. I was there one Friday when Chris, the pub heaving with custom, was summoned to do the necessary, and with desperate irony asked, 'What's the problem, Bob, floor filled up, is it?'

Bob was impervious. 'I can always go elsewhere,' he said.

'Feel free,' Chris told him.

But Bob's leer indicated an unshakeable confidence in the landlord's acceptance of his behaviour.

He was right. Chris, a man who kept an orderly house, rarely barred anyone from his door. He didn't need to. He had a natural authority about him, tolerant but not to be put upon. He was someone we all liked, and though we were less certain of Bob, and from time to time several drinkers reckoned his glowering, sullen presence turned their ale sour, there was no getting rid of him.

Now, holding up an empty packet of Player's for my inspection, Chris said, 'That's him. That's Bob. Likes to throw something away when he leaves. Makes him Lord of the Manor.'

Half an hour later I repeated Chris's words to Harold as we rumbled along to Bingham in his battered camper van, on the side of which was written **HOUSE CLEARANCES** and, underneath, *Smaller articles considered*. Harold was wearing an old but well-preserved grey suit, collar and tie. Harold Burchfield businessman, together with his assistant in brown cord jacket, sweater and jeans.

'Yeh,' Harold said. 'It's Bob's way of showing that he's not your ordinary worker.'

'Bob? What is he, then? I mean, what's he do, exactly? I thought he was on Player's shop floor.'

'Tell him that and he'd have a heart attack.' Harold's laugh was more of a bark. 'Either that, or he'd trample on you.'

'He's got the feet for it,' I agreed. Bob wore enormous, highly polished brogues, size fourteen at the least. 'What's he do for a living then?'

Harold didn't reply until we'd turned off the main road. 'Keep your eyes skinned,' he then said. 'We're looking for Manor Farm. A couple of miles on, according to the directions I was given.'

For a few minutes we drove in silence as Harold steered us along a rutted lane, hedges high on both sides – 'Be just my luck to meet a tractor coming at us, and I'll be the poor sod who has to back up' – before he said, 'Bob's a gate manager. That's what he calls himself, any road. Mr. Big, to hear him talk. Checks vehicles in and out. Has to phone ahead to tell, warn, store foremen a new supply is on its way. Paper, tobacco leaf, cardboard, whatever you need to make cigarettes and package them up, I suppose.'

'I see.'

'Buggered if I do,' Harold said. 'I guess he stands by the front gate with his cap on making life difficult for everyone. Listening to his blather you'd reckon that without him the factory wouldn't survive. Treats himself as a – sorry, *the,* Company Director. He gets a hundred free smokes a month, so he says. From a grateful company. '

'Is that why he always wears a suit and tie in the Oak? I've often wondered.'

'And why he drinks bottled brown ale,' Harold said, laughing. 'And raises his pinkie when he puts the glass to his lips. And votes Tory. Hey up, we're here. Manor Farm.'

Once we were through the farm gates, Harold stopped in front of the farmhouse itself, and I sat there while he went inside. He was gone for some while, no doubt giving the goods he was after the once over, presumably haggling over the price. When he reappeared in the doorway, it was to give me the thumbs up.

For the best part of an hour we worked together, bringing out a dresser, a chest of drawers, two rolls of carpet, plus a single mattress that we heaved up on to the van's roof before covering it in a tarpaulin which we secured with rope in a manner Harold had taught me to use on previous jaunts. Reef knot, clove hitch, slip knot … I never remembered the names but under Harold's tutelage I learnt how to tie them. Then there were the cartons of crockery, some cutlery, a heavy box of glassware. By the time we were done my arms and shoulders were aching, and I wished I'd remembered to bring a pair of gloves with me.

But Harold was fresh as paint. 'Nice little haul, this lot,' he said as we made our way back to Nottingham. 'Should fetch a penny or two.'

'How did you hear about it?'

Harold was a great reader of *Exchange & Mart* but this seemed different from his usual dealings. I'd been with him – 'riding shotgun' he called it – on occasions when he'd gone in search of old batteries, lawnmowers, garden tools, tin plates, camping equipment … any old iron. On Saturdays when I was free for an hour or so, I'd go off with Harold in his van and watch him hard-bargaining for goods which, once he'd settled on a price, we'd pile into the van and then bring back to the lock-up beside his house where I'd help him unload. But what we now had aboard was definitely more up-market. Was Harold raising his game?

'The *Post's* Small Ads.' Harold said. We were following a flat-bed lorry into Nottingham, its trailer swaying with the parts of what looked like a merry-go-round. 'That's where to look for bargains when folks are selling up.' He looked across at me. 'There's a fair amount of that at the moment. Folk selling up and moving on.'

He pointed to the lorry ahead of us.

'That's not from a house sale,' I said.

Harold laughed. No,' he said, 'Goose Fair, that is.'

For some minutes we drove in silence, then Harold said, 'We'd not have been able to do this next weekend. Streets will be clogged for miles around.'

'Do you plan on going?'

Harold swung out and round the lorry, then slowed so we could take the Derby bypass.

Then, 'Goose Fair?' he said, 'I'm bit long in the tooth for that.' 'You?' he asked. And, answering his own question, 'No, I suppose not. Not really for a college lecturer.'

'We'll be there,' I said. 'The kids will want us to take them. Anyway, I like the dodgems. I think Pauline's arranged to bring some friends' children along. We'll stay until they've spent all their pocket money and then we'll go for a fish and chip supper. It's fun for them. Trouble is, it always rains on Goose Fair.'

It didn't, but still.

'Children,' Harold said. 'First they break your arm then they break your heart.'

I looked across at him and he was smiling, a small, sad smile. Almost as though speaking to himself, he said, 'That's what I heard. I wouldn't know. I never had any.' He was staring at the road ahead. 'We wanted kids but it never happened and in the end we gave up trying. And now I'm on my own with no one to leave the Burchfield millions to, not a soul.'

Then why bother to make more money? I wanted to ask, and as though I'd spoken aloud, Harold said, 'Habit of a lifetime.'

We drove in silence for some minutes until a roundabout came up where Harold steered left onto a tree-lined boulevard and we saw the familiar buildings to our right, screened by poplars, the buildings Lawrence had called Sir Jesse Boot's 'cakey university'.

'Nearly home,' I said.

'And after we've stashed this lot, we're due a beer or two. I'm paying.'

'Thanks,' I said.

'How's your good lady?' Harold asked. It was a formal enquiry. 'Pauline? She's fine.'

'She wasn't with you last night.'

'No,' I said, 'She's taken our two to Bournemouth for a long weekend, to stay with her parents.'

I wondered whether to say more, but decided not to. He'd not be interested. Harold and I were on friendly enough terms but there was an inevitable gap between us. I knew he'd been left a widower some years before we arrived in Beeston, but he never told me anything about his late wife. And why should he? He kept his loneliness to himself. We waved to each other, I sometimes thought, across an unbridgeable gulf. I didn't like that any more, I hoped, than did Harold. But it was there. I liked him, enjoyed his company, was always pleased to see him in the Oak, enjoyed riding shotgun for him; but beyond that ... well, beyond that, I don't know.

We were on Villa Street now, passing the pub, its street door open, and, then, a few yards further on, we came to a halt outside the lock-up at the end of the short terrace where Harold lived. The house was a two-storey up-and-downer that Harold, so those who had been inside remarked, kept in spotless condition.

'I'll open up,' he said.

Cutting the ignition, he levered back his door and made to climb down from the driver's seat. But then, turning back, he said, 'Thanks for your help, mate. I appreciate it.'

'No sweat,' I told him. 'Always at your disposal, as you know. Unless Pauline and I are due to dine with Lord and Lady Muck.'

Harold forgave the clumsy attempt at humour. 'If you need to borrow any gold plate,' he said, 'Tell my butler and he'll see you right. No charge.'

It took us some time to empty the van's contents and stash everything in Harold's lock-up. As with house, at least according to report, so with lock-up.

'I like to keep everything shipshape,' he'd said the first time I stood in that dark cave, and when he snapped on the overhead light I could see at a glance what he meant.

'All for sale,' he explained, as I stared around at collections of garden tools, at wheelbarrows leaning up against the back wall, at a stack of car batteries, mounds of car tyres, of kitchen utensils ranged along shelves, beside them neat piles of crockery, of clocks of all sorts and sizes, even long-case, of sets of hard-back chairs. 'Mine eyes dazzle,' I said. Harold ignored my words. 'Piece of advice,' he said. 'If you ever find yourself in my line of business and planning to invite a punter in for a look-see, just make sure the place is all spick-and-span. For why? Because, my son, it creates a favourable impression, a serious, buying-and-selling atmosphere. Joe Public sniffs the air and thinks, 'Ah, this bloke's a professional, a man to be trusted, only handles kosher material. See, that way you don't need to haggle. "This is what I'm selling at, take it or leave it, but don't waste my time or yours thinking you can beat me down.'"

As he talked he was walking about the lock-up, straightening up pieces of furniture as he did so. 'My old dad taught me that. "Keep your sale-room in good order, Harold," he told me, "and you won't need to bargain over the asking price. Haggle over what you'll pay but *never* haggle over what you're selling. Leave that to your average totter. And never call your place of work your junk yard. It's your office.'"

Harold shook his head as he laughed at the memory of those words. 'My old dad, he drove a horse and cart all round Nottingham. Big streets and little. Sneinton or The Park. It was all the same to him. "Bring out what you've got to sell. A Fair price for Fair Goods." I cheeked him once, called him a rag-and-bone man. I got a real leatherin' for that. Never again.'

Now, as we stood outside Harold's 'office', after he'd locked up and while we were dusting ourselves down, I asked, 'Do you invite people in here to look over the goods?' I'd always puzzled over how Harold did business. He didn't have a board outside the lock-up, and yet whenever I went in I could see at a glance that since my previous visit some goods had gone, others were newly arrived.

'I do. It's all a matter of word of mouth. That's the way to advertise. Don't pay for it. With this stuff we got from Bingham I'll do what I always do, watch me. Into the Oak, let drop I've got some good new furniture and all 'classy'. No need to overdo it, a hint's better than a headline. They'll be round here before you can say Jack shit. Pauline might well take a fancy to that dresser, for instance.'

'I'll ask her,' I said, none too seriously.

'You do that,' Harold said, checking the padlock was snapped shut. 'Right' he said, as he forced a large bunch of keys into his trouser pocket. 'A good morning's work, that is, for which

I reckon you're owed a pint or two of Chris's finest. So quick march, young man. And remember, I'm paying.'

3: Sheffield Tommy's Enemy

'Hallo,' Harold said, 'What's goin' on here, then? Chris dealing drugs on the side?'

A police car, blue roof-light flashing, blocked the narrow road directly in front of the pub's street door.

He led the way inside.

At this hour on a Saturday the place was usually full, the constant hubbub of laughter and talk charged with the atmosphere unique to the day and the time, an expectant, eye-bright thrill of something about to happen. Men and women, not all husbands and wives, treating themselves to a lunchtime drink after their morning's shopping, others who'd come off half-day shift at one or other of the local lace factories, still in their overalls, and now, free from work until Monday, grouped together in festive rowdiness. Still others, for the most part younger drinkers, readying themselves for an afternoon in the city, where they'd be meeting friends in Slab Square or at Colwick if horse-racing was on, or planning to join other football supporters at Meadow Lane, on the city side of the Trent where County played, or make for the City Ground, home to Forest on the farther, county side of the river; or, at a guess, some to head for sessions at the ice-rink, or for window-shopping at the Victoria Centre, the city's new, covered shopping mall.

But on this occasion the pub was quiet, and though both Public and Saloon bars held their fair share of regulars, there was little by way of talk and none of the raucously cheerful hubbub that characterised Saturday lunchtime in The Royal Oak.

At the end of the passage, back turned to the newcomers, a tall, uniformed policeman was in earnest conversation with Chris.

He turned as Harold and I approached the bar.

'Everything alright?' Harold asked, which it plainly wasn't, and 'Hallo, Adam,' I said. 'What brings you here?'

Our enquiries were met by a stiff nod. Then, relaxing a little, the policeman said to me 'So this is where you drink when not on the cricket field.' But still, there was a watchful look about him. A policeman on duty can't afford to let his guard down. Besides, the last time we'd met I'd bowled Adam Frith out when he thought himself well set, and as a result of that freak delivery, as Frith at least was convinced it had been, denied South Notts Police their expected victory against the University Staff Eleven.

'You two gents know each other, then,' Chris said, looking startled and, then, relieved.

'Through cricket,' I said, adding 'Adam here – Sergeant Frith – is an excellent batsman. It takes an even better bowler to winkle him out.'

Frith was not amused. Speaking in professional mode, he said, 'I'm here because we're pursuing enquiries into the circumstances surrounding a death.' He paused. 'That's why.'

Harold and I looked to Chris for enlightenment, but before he could say anything, Frith spoke again. 'A Mister Thomas Burton,' he said.

'What, Sheffield Tommy? He's *dead?*'

And when Frith nodded, Harold asked, 'When? Where? How? He was in here last night,' he added.

'We know,' Frith said. ' A pause. 'And we know where he died and we know, more or less, when the death occurred.'

'But how?'

Frith looked at me, every inch the policeman. 'The circumstances of his death were, shall we say, suspicious.'

'You mean *murder?*' Harold and I spoke together. We could sense that drinkers in the two bars had fallen quiet, and were now listening to what was being said in the passage.

As though sensing he might have said too much, Frith gave ground. 'It's the assumption we're working on.'

Harold and I looked at each other, mystified, then across to Chris. But his expression was blank. Not a clue, it said.

'Do either of you gentlemen know this Mister Burton?'

'Of course we do,' Harold said, 'Everybody knows him. There's no harm in Sheffield Tommy, I'll tell you that.'

'And were you in here last evening? If so can you verify that you saw Mister Burton?'

'Yes to both questions,' Harold said. 'Tommy's in here every Friday night. And when he's in there's no missing him.'

Frith turned to Chris. 'Is there somewhere quiet we can go?' he asked. 'I'd like to interview these gentlemen and then call in others, ask a few questions.' He turned to us. 'It's either that or the police station. And I imagine you'd prefer here.'

'Much prefer,' Harold said, and Chris, speaking over him, announced, 'The Snug, that'll do you.' He came out from behind his bar, led the way across the passage to a small room which Margaret used for drying her weekly wash, and opening the door, said, 'You'll be OK here.'

Apart from a wooden clothes horse on which hung a voluminous pair of woollen underpants, the little room was empty.

'Will these disturb you?' Chris asked, looking round at us all. 'They're mine.'

'Not worth much on the open market,' Harold said.

'I'll leave you to it, then.' Ignoring Harold's pleasantry, our landlord stepped back into the passage, about to shut the door behind him when Frith ordered him to tell others in the pub he'd want to speak to them. 'Anyone who has to leave, make sure you take down their details. Names, addresses….'

Waiting until Chris had closed the door, and then, as though wishing to shield the underpants from general view, Adam Frith took up position in front of the clothes horse. 'Right,' he said, 'Now, let's start with your names and occupations.'

'Don't you want to know what time we left here last night?' Harold asked.

Careful, Harold, I wanted to tell him. I know Frith. He won't take kindly to any lip.

The policeman gave Harold what he no doubt intended as a measured look. 'Names, current addresses, and occupations.'

I gave my name, which of course Frith knew perfectly well, added my address, and Harold identified himself as Harold Burchfield, described himself as a dealer in domestic appliances and furnishings, and gave his address: 39 Villa Street, Beeston.

'And you were both in here last evening?'

We nodded.

'Until closing time?'

More nodding.

'And you observed the deceased leave the premises.'

'And heard him,' Harold said.

The policeman said, 'And the last you saw of him was when he left.'

'Yes,' I said, and Harold nodded agreement. Then he repeated his earlier question. 'So what had poor old Tommy been doing?'

'It's what's been done to him that concerns me.'

Rocking slightly on the balls of his feet, Frith flipped over the pages of his notebook and in a voice that suggested he might be reading the shipping forecast intoned, 'At twelve-thirty a.m. on the night of Sept. 28th, 1971, a man was discovered lying face down on the steps leading up to a block of flats at Hyson Green.' He paused in order to turn the page. 'A passer-by tried to arouse him, but noticing blood coming from the top of his head called the police. A patrol car was dispatched from Canning Circus Police Station and arrived on the scene some fifteen minutes later.'

Frith closed his notebook. 'There's more,' he said, 'but that gives you the general picture.'

'Not really,' Harold said. 'Did he fall or was he pushed? Accident or not? He'd had his usual skinful when he left here …. And by the way, how did you know he'd been in the Royal Oak last evening?'

Frith gave him a look that was part complacent, part contemptuous. 'House to house enquiries. Or in this case pub to pub,' he said. 'Four of us on the job, it took less than an hour.'

'And no doubt somebody where he lived had a good idea of his movements. A creature of habit, old Tommy. Still,' Harold shook his head, 'a sod of a way to go.' Then, 'How do you know it wasn't an accident? He might have slipped on the steps.'

'It was no accident,' Adam Frith said. 'He'd been hit by a blunt object on the back of his head. We got him to hospital pronto but he was confirmed d.o.a. Whoever hit him meant business.' But then he stopped. Once again, he had to guard against saying too much.

'Poor Tommy,' I said, and Harold said, 'Poor bloke, he wouldn't say boo to a goose. He didn't deserve to end up dead, not like that, anyway.'

There were a few more questions, but Frith, I could see, knew we were of no help to him in his enquiries, and soon we were out of the Snug and free to contemplate our long overdue pint.

But it came to me that I didn't want one, not now, not in view of what we'd been told about Tommy, and I could tell that Harold felt the same way.

We parted at the doorway of the pub. 'This evening, perhaps,' Harold said, but his heart wasn't in it.

***

At home I made myself a cheese sandwich and must have chewed it standing up, though when I looked at my empty plate I'd no memory of having eaten. I was thinking of Tommy, of what always seemed his indefatigable cheerfulness, and I was remembering that phrase of his, 'The enemy is out of sight'. I knew where it came from. When I was a small boy my mother used to sing to me as I got ready for bed, one of those sentimental American songs of the nineteen-thirties that infuriatingly sticks in the memory and which, as a result, I carried into adulthood. There's a version of it, of the tune at least, by Ruby Braff, the American cornet player, that brings out the melody's odd, plaintive beauty. By all accounts Braff was a difficult customer, surly, combative, a loner. The story goes that one New Year he and another New York musician passed each other on their ways to different gigs. 'Happy New Year, Ruby,' the other musician called out. Braff glared at him. 'Nobody tells me what kind of new year to have,' he said.

Apocryphal, no doubt, but I'm not alone in thinking that any instinct for emotional warmth Braff had went into his playing, its unique, lyric warmth. Anyway, in that song, which is called, I think, 'Little Man, You've Had a Busy Day,' the singer is a father or mother consoling a small son for the fact that someone has stolen away his kiddie car, but reassuring him that 'the enemy is out of sight' and as a result it's safe 'to go to sleep now.'

Did the infant Tommy Burton's father or mother once sing that song to their son? Not very likely. Indeed, I soon realised, out of the question. Tommy had fought in the war, which meant that he must have been at the very least in his late teenage years when he became part of Montgomery's Eighth Army. If so, he'd have been born in the early nineteen-twenties, and I was pretty sure that the song came on the market in the mid to late nineteen-thirties. 'Little Man?' Cosseted by parental care, breathing love into his soul. No, forget it. That was pure indulgence on my part. Tommy's cheerfulness, the fact that everybody I knew who had come across him – during his kitchen duties or pub peregrinations – plainly liked him, that and the jaunty walk, the would-be stylish outfit, the delight in singing, the battered face with its watery blue eyes whose brightness never dimmed, were natural to him, *were* him.

But then I thought, you don't really know that. What happens when he's on his own, in his bedsit? And I began to imagine a life for him of a loneliness he couldn't cure. And Larkin's poem about Mr Bleaney's room came into my head, those lines in which the poet imagines how Bleaney might lie on his bed thinking that 'how we live measures our own nature,/ And at his age having no more to show/Than one hired room should make him sure/He warranted no better.' A life of quiet desperation. Was it for this the clay grew tall? Well, then, thank goodness for pubs and the hours they gave of sociability, of at least temporary companionship.

Anyway, I had work to do, a book to write, lectures to prepare. And, far more important, I had a wife and children who would be home tomorrow and I wanted to discuss over a meal with Pauline the death of Tommy Burton, and, before that, hear from the children about the delights of their half-term visit to grandparents who would no doubt have spoilt them something rotten.

4: Beeston at the Flicks

When I stepped into the Oak next noon, Chris, who was just removing the towels from his beer handles, said, 'Well, well, I didn't expect to see you just yet. I had you down for a more civilised hour.'

'I'm not stopping, landlord,' I said. 'I'm after a couple of bottles of pale ale, then I'll be on my way.'

Chris was in his Sunday best. A maroon V-necked sweater, plus yellow, polka-dot cravat, and, though I couldn't see them from where he stood behind the bar, I knew his legs would be encased in a pair of immaculate grey trousers and on his feet he'd have highly-polished brown brogues. Everyone who came into the pub for Sunday lunchtime took care over their appearances. Men in suits, women with hair coiffed from Saturday visits to the hairdresser, in coats or jackets to which were pinned brooches or nosegays.

Reaching for the bottles beneath the bar counter, Chris said, as he straightened up, 'Seems the Boys in Blue have already got Tommy's killers.'

'Killers? With an *s*? How many did it take to murder him then?' And then, 'And how do you know, if I may ask?'

'It was on the Nine o'clock news.'

He meant Radio Nottingham, of course. Chris, like many of his regulars, only listened to the local news, as he only read the daily *Nottingham Post*.

'That didn't take long. What did the killers do, walk into the local station, give themselves up?'

I wasn't sure how seriously I intended my words, but Chris said, 'That's about the size of it. A couple of teenagers, drunk out of their heads, they meant no harm, or so the reporter said, asked poor old Tommy to stop singing and when he wouldn't they pushed him to the ground. He landed on his head and they ran off. No idea they'd done him any harm.'

'So how did they find out?'

'According to the radio the police were on a door-to-door fast enough, knocking up locals. Our likely lads were woken from their sleep in the early hours and on their way to Canning Circus before you could say Jack Robinson.'

'There must be more to it than that,' I said, paying for my ale.

'There will be,' Chris said. 'A full report in tomorrow's *Post*, no doubt. But that's the gist of it. Poor Tommy, poor bugger. Knocked over and done in by a pair of drunken louts.'

'I suppose there'll be a funeral?'

'Though goodness knows who'll arrange or pay for it,' Chris said. 'I don't suppose he had a bean, and probably no family, either. Leastways, I never heard tell of relatives.'

He looked past me, his face now wearing a regulation smile, and I turned to see a couple I vaguely knew coming through the street door.

'Good day, Hilda, my dear,' Chris said with formal joviality to the middle-aged woman who was already turning into the Public Bar. And as she smiled at him, he said, 'You'll be taking your usual, I expect, and this rogue you can't shake off will no doubt want his regular pint. Is that so, James?'

Jim Philimore, an electrician at one of the local lace factories, blue serge suit straining to sheathe his bulky body, Brylcreemed hair fissured by a central parting, winked at Chris. 'A glass of your best gnats-piss will do for me,' he said. 'Clear the pipes so I can enjoy my dinner.'

'What will you be tucking into, then?'

'Leg of pork,' Philimore told Chris, who I was sure didn't care and who was never at his best when having to play the part of Mine Host. But he had to pretend an interest, if only because his wife, so I'd heard, was related to one of Beeston's butchers.

Walking home, bottles in a carrier bag, I tried to remember which butcher Margaret claimed kinship with, but without success. At that time the town had enough custom to support three butchers. Half-way down the High Street was one called, unbelievably, Hogg. Further along, toward the university end, the other two businesses stood almost side by side. *Albert Marlow &*

Son, Fine Meats and *Pritchards, Pork Butchers,* were separated by a shop which sold or failed to sell stationery. Pritchards, from where the Philimores' leg of pork almost certainly came, made a good deal of its money from faggots. I didn't much like faggots but they were reckoned a delicacy by workers from the local lace factories who bought them on their way home after completing the day's shift. Faggots were a concoction of minced pork and lard, rolled into the size of snooker balls, highly seasoned with pepper, and fried so as to be ready for sale and warm when they were bought. A large metal jug of thick brown gravy stood on the counter and workers who brought with them their own bowl or tray could have gravy poured over their faggots to complete the pleasure. Most, though, made do with having their purchase rolled in newspaper which some pushed inside their jackets or overalls or, even, shirts, before cycling away.

All of Beeston's lace factories are long since shut, and Pritchards' shop vanished years ago. But for a long time it was reckoned to be the best pork butchers for miles around.

My own favourite butcher, though, was Albert Marlow. This was partly, I suppose, because he looked the part. Round faced, portly, with a straw hat perched on top of his sleek black hair, always with a line in badinage that bordered on the comical and/or obscurely erotic. 'Here y'are, then Mrs Hopkins, these kidneys will fill your husband's pouch for you,' and Mrs Hopkins, a stout seventy-year-old with a husband known for his 'medical difficulties' (aka incontinence), would smile complicitly as she pushed the wrapped parcel into her large leather shopping bag and left the shop, straw-bonneted head held high. Or, 'A pound of sausages for you, is it, Mrs Gregson? Would you like me to slip you an extra one?' And the waiting queue would smirk among themselves while Mrs Gregson attempted a dignified exit, barely acknowledging her friends.

A high-legged chair, placed at the far end of the counter, provided a seat for a succession of old familiars who would park themselves on it in order to pass the time of day not merely with Albert but with his customers. Other shops along the high street had such chairs, all of them occupied by ageing citizens prepared to announce that they were there because they were 'just passing, can't stop,' and who, half-an-hour or so later, as they levered themselves up from the chair, would say 'Well, must get on,' or 'No rest for the wicked,' or 'Time and Tide wait for No Man,' or 'I'll have to be on my way, the wife (or old man) will wonder where I've got to,' or any one of a variety of phrases, each and every one of them suggesting that the speaker had no time at all to spare, but that civility demanded he or she couldn't pass the open door (even if it was closed) without paying his, or her, respects.

But Albert Marlow's chair was top seat in Beeston. His shop accordingly was where you went, I was told, if you wanted the latest, or juiciest gossip. As sociological linguists might say, the shop was a site for the study of idiomatic utterance, distinguished by both verbal and visual expressivity. In other – and better – words, it was where you went for what the Irish call 'crack'.

Wonder, incredulity, outrage, contempt – 'he never did', 'she won't be able to show *her* face again,' 'well, good luck to them I say,' – these and other such remarks, accompanied by snorts, eye-rolling, head-shaking, heavy sighs, the whole gallimaufry of people pleasure could be found – heard and seen – among Albert Marlow's regulars.

I wasn't a regular but whenever I went into his shop I expected to be entertained, and I wasn't often disappointed. Standing in line, waiting to be served, and all the time listening in to the talk, I was reminded of a radio comedian called Al Reed, who during the nineteen- fifties, when I was in my very early teens, became a favourite on BBC Light Programme variety shows. He claimed to have begun life as a butcher – in Leeds I think – who got most of his material from listening to his customers' talk. I can well believe it. Radio comics in the nineteen-forties and early fifties, of whom there were many, relied on catch phrases. It was a way of making yourself distinct from the others. 'Don't forget the diver'; 'It's being so cheerful that keeps me going', (dolefully spoken by a character called Mona Lott); 'The day war broke out' (Rob Wilton's words of introduction to one of his shaggy-dog stories), and others. Two of Al Reed's catch phrases have stayed with me for over sixty years. 'I thought, Right Monkey' (an overheard woman planning on how to get even with someone who's riled her) and the supreme, 'There was enough said at our Edie's wedding', as a way of cutting off sharp-tongued rumour. Even the Goons had a number of such phrases, including several that became part of the currency of playground life. 'You have deaded me', 'He's fallen in the water,' 'Nobody's perfect' (Eccles' protest at being told that as a ship's navigator he's four thousand miles off course and in the middle of a desert.) And then there was one that especially delighted my mother. It featured in *Just William,* a series of tales drawn from Richmal Crompton's stories and adapted for tea-time radio. I can't remember which afternoon it was on, but I do remember that for each occasion she, my sister and myself gathered round the wireless, agog for the moment when the errand boy would call out to William 'How's your mother off for dripping?' The words never failed to draw hoots of laughter from our mother, laughter in which Jill and I would obligingly join.

All gone now, of course, those radio shows, as have the chairs at shops' counters, as have the shops themselves. Now most people shop at supermarkets – and the queues at check-out rarely spark conversation, after all, the queuers are invariably strangers to each other – or they shop on-line. No talk there. No chance to report that 'There was enough said at our Edie's wedding.'

***

Albert Marlow &Son, Fine Meats closed up some time in the nineteen-eighties, but not before Albert had experienced a moment of fame. I heard about it later, and it probably became burnished in re-telling, but the fact of it was wonder enough. Because Albert Marlow, butcher of Beeston, featured in a film. He was on the big screen, there for all to see. A man with a world-wide reputation. Sort of.

How did it happen? It's a tale fit for his high chair and this is the gist of it.

Sometime in the early nineteen-sixties one of Albert Marlow's regular customers went with her husband to see whatever was that week's Star Attraction at Nottingham's Odeon. In those days, cinema programmes were still made up of what were called A and B Features. The B Feature was a short film, as a rule lasting less than an hour, usually shot in black-and-white, and 'starring' actors of reliable incompetence. As for the plots, such as they were, these involved the unmasking of criminals who had – say – made off with money or goods that didn't belong to them, or who for some reason never explained chose to kidnap a young woman wearing a tight white sweater and a blank expression.

Among the criminals Freddie Mills often appeared, either 'as himself' or in a supporting role, in which case he'd be called 'Butch' or 'Buster'. And who, I hear you ask, was Mills? The answer is that he had been rescued from life as a milk roundsman by discovering that he had some talent as a boxer, and in fact became briefly world light-heavyweight champion. However, in his subsequent career as a heavyweight he was regularly knocked out by visiting American bruisers in 'title fights' of dubious authenticity. He was thus classed on back pages as 'sporting,' 'gallant,' or even 'heroic,' and over time he came to possess what the dailies liked to call 'craggy features'. These gained him parts in B Feature films in which he was never allowed to say more than 'Right Boss,' or 'He won't get away with it,' not so much because he couldn't act, though he couldn't, but because he would be unlikely to remember a longer speech. The hero of these films, whether Private Eye or Good Citizen, was played by one or the other of two American 'actors', Paul Carpenter or Oscar Bonaventura Jnr. Quite why an American detective should be present in what was supposed to be London's East End was never explained, probably because it was beyond explanation, but the film invariably ended in a car crash which killed the villains, or a chase through an empty factory where the chief villain climbed up a fire-escape and then fell off or ran along a rooftop with the same result. 'Run' is, needless to say, something of an exaggeration. Spavined stagger would be nearer the mark.

But then, as A Features became longer, so the need for such classics of unqualified ineptitude disappeared. As it happened, B Features vanished from screens at the moment when Bonaventura, together with Carpenter, who wasn't a bad singer and who had occasionally worked with the excellent Ted Heath Orchestra, were killed in a late night car crash.

Still, film distributors sensed the need for something to take the place of B Features, something shorter, of course, but nevertheless something to fill the gap between adverts and the A Feature, that space during which toilets could be visited and ice creams bought. The warm-up spot, so to speak, was now filled by increasing numbers of trailers for 'forthcoming attractions' and by other short 'features', all-too-often including a Technicolor travelogue of ten minutes' duration called, 'Look at Life'. The format for this never changed. A wide-angled camera homes in on a spot – a city, a landscape, an island – while a voice intones some kind of welcome, and, then, following ten minutes of vacuous commentary, the camera draws back, it is sunset, and the voice announces 'And so we say Farewell to …' wherever.

One of these Looks at Life was about Cyprus and it was this which a couple of Albert Marlow's regular customers saw on a visit to the Odeon. Not surprisingly, they were transfixed by a moment when the camera followed a pair of lovers as they walked hand-in-hand along a beach, the man gripping a plastic bag on which in large white and blue lettering was written, for all the world to see, *Albert Marlow & Son, Fine Meats Beeston.*

Back from the Odeon, the couple 'just popped in' to tell Albert their news. Albert, who was shutting up shop for the day, at once summoned a taxi and managed to get to the Odeon in time for the evening performance. The next day a thirty-seater coach was ordered, and favoured customers were offered a free trip to the Odeon *and* free tickets in order to see 'Look at Life'. They were thus able to witness for themselves the evidence of Albert Marlow's stardom.

Asked later what the A Feature had been like Albert reputedly answered, 'Buggered if I know.'

5: The Man of Knowledge

Several of the Oak's drinkers accepted Albert Marlow's offer of a free trip to the Odeon, though most claimed to have left as the sun set on Cyprus. They wanted to be back on home territory before Chris called 'time'. Bob, who had of course kept to his corner, claimed indifference if not downright contempt for modern films. 'All the same, all of them,' he said.

'I don't see how you could have seen any,' someone reportedly challenged him. 'You're always in here by seven o'clock.'

'Don't need to see them,' Bob said. 'They're all the bloody same.'

Writing about his own local pub in the south country, The Compasses, Nicholas Shakespeare surmises that like other local hostelries, 'The Compasses came into being out of our need to come together, not merely to fraternise but, loosened by ale, to intellectualise and philosophise …. Before the medieval traveller who stepped inside was dangled the intoxicating promise of having revealed to him "new facts in other branches of knowledge outside his ken" ….' I don't imagine Bob would allow anything to be beyond his ken, and if it was it certainly wouldn't be of interest. He was what could charitably be called a know-all.

I suppose all pubs once had their resident know-alls. No, let me amend that. I imagine that all pubs counted among their regulars certain men – never, I think, women – who appointed themselves to be what their fellow drinkers might call wiseacres. It's an interesting word, wiseacre. The OED dates it to the late sixteenth century. 'A pretender to wisdom; a foolish person with an air or affectation of wisdom; a know-all.' The same dictionary also provides 'A wise or learned person, a sage. Chiefly *derog*. M18' But why wiseacre? Acres wide? Not so long ago there was a fashion of referring to knowledgeable men – *and* women (we live in enlightened times) – as possessing brains the size of Kent. I've no idea why Kent was chosen for this bizarre comparison. It's by no means the largest of English counties. And in outline the county doesn't look at all like a crammed skull. Essex does, but of course Essex is associated with a particular kind of numbskullery. Anyway, like that phrenological rage of the nineteenth century, the fashion came and went. And as for 'wiseacre', I've not heard the term for years, probably not since about the time the Oak closed its door for the last time.

But it's good to know that, according to Brewer's *Dictionary of Phrase and Fable,* the term, which the dictionary notes is a corruption of the German *weissager* (a sage or prophet), is in English associated with pub or tavern life. Hence, the following entry.

> There is a story told that Ben Jonson, at the *Devil's Tavern* in Fleet Street, said to a gentleman who boasted of his country estates, 'What care we for your dirt and clods? Where you have an acre of land I have ten acres of wit.' The gentleman retorted by calling Ben 'Good Mr Wiseacre.'

Big Bob was a man of dirt and clods, and proud of it. Quite a few of the Oak's regulars rented allotment strips at the nearby 'Community Gardens', and worked on their patches during summer evenings and at weekends. They would from time to time arrive at the pub carrying bags to show off and/or sell the fruits of their labour. I wasn't alone in buying cabbages, cauliflowers, runner beans, carrots and potatoes from one or other of the growers. Their produce was reliably good.

Not according to Big Bob, though. 'Call that a potato? The only reason it hasn't got wire-worm is that it's too bloody small to give the buggers house room.' Or, 'That's never a cauli. More like a toadstool.'

The put-downs were perhaps intended as jovial, but there was an edge to them. From his seat beside the hearth, Bob dispensed judgement as if speaking from the clouds. He of course did not rent his own allotment strip. He let it be known that he had a back garden bigger, better, more fruitful, than any such strip. He didn't therefore need to carry his tools to and fro. They were ready to hand. As was his wife, who supplied cups of tea and sandwiches on demand.

On Sundays, we were given to understand, the tea arrived at eleven-thirty sharp, allowing him time for an hour's further toil before he shook the earth from his boots and went indoors 'for a shit and a shave,' after which he put on his Sunday trousers and shirt, and was ready to take himself to the Oak. Regulars who were unlucky enough to be within earshot were given a run-down of Bob's Sundays, from the moment he rose, at eight o'clock, smoked his first cigarette of the day, then took himself into breakfast. Breakfast was unvarying, we would be pleased to know. Two fried eggs, four rashers of bacon ('not Pritchards' bloody rammel, either, the wife gets ours from Hogg's, best back, cut thick, he knows who it's for), a couple of tomatoes, home-grown and therefore extra large, and half-a-dozen blueys. (Blueys were extra large flat mushrooms rumoured to hide maggots; you could buy them at local greengrocers, and many did, though I think they've now disappeared.) Two cups of tea, another fag, and it was then time to set about the vegetable garden where produce of unparalleled size and beauty could be annually guaranteed.

Despite occasional requests, Bob never produced any of these products for our admiring gaze. Not even Arthur Crouch was allowed a viewing. Arthur, an auxiliary fireman, seemed to divide his time between the town's fire station and the Oak. A very short, hump-backed man with a long, sharp nose and half of one ear seemingly bitten off (rumours that he'd lost it during a passionate encounter with the fire station cleaner were not widely believed), Arthur was the only one of the regulars prepared to sit with Bob and listen to his bombastic ramblings. He said little beyond 'Oh, aye,' whenever it seemed that Bob had completed an observation on world affairs. 'This bloody government, no good for anything bar taxing hard-working people like me.' 'Oh, aye.' 'The thing about brown ale is, you can rely on it tasting the same, year in, year out, not like the swill most of you lot drink.' 'Oh, aye.' Or. 'What's the point of the television, there's never anything worth watching, not even the bloody adverts.' 'Oh, aye.' Or, 'I said to the wife only yesterday that if Hitler were still alive he'd walk straight into the country; all these long-haired layabouts, they don't know which end of a rifle to hold. If I had my way they'd be locked up or sent back to where they came from. No use to man nor beast. Not like us when we was young. We had some fire in our bellies.' 'Oh, aye.'

This last observation nearly led Bob into trouble. It was overheard by a regular who always stood in the passage, someone known to have fought at Dunkirk. Putting down his drink, the man, named, I think, Frank Ennis, came into the Lounge Bar and stood over the table where Bob sat. 'Tell us what you did in the war, then, you fat berk. Stayed well out of it, so I heard. Under the bed, most of the time, hiding from the MPs.'

The words silenced Bob, for a few minutes at least, and after Ennis had gone back to his beer, you could see Bob glancing around the room, wondering how much we'd overheard. Sometime later I heard that Bob had in fact been in army uniform, though there was little agreement as to exactly how he'd helped the war effort. Assistant quartermaster at Chilwell? Jankers wallah? ARP Warden?

He wasn't a likeable man, Bob, and I was always surprised to discover that his wife, a small, neatly-dressed woman with a sad expression, seemed fond of him. At all events, on the very few occasions I saw them together in public – out for a stroll along the High Street more often than not – her arm was through his and she was ready to smile agreement whenever he opened his mouth to speak.

Bob was the archetypal wiseacre. You looked at him and you thought of Bounderby and of Podsnap rolled up together into one gross body. Like all wiseacres he did his best to silence opposition. Should Arthur have dared to mount a protest against any of Bob's plodding generalisations – though he never did – he'd have been met by the words Bob threw out at anyone who dared to take him on: 'That's all *you* know.'

But there was one habitué of the Saloon Bar before whom Bob, as it were, kept his head down. Ian – I regret I never knew his surname – was in most lunchtimes, so I gathered, and returned most evenings. At lunchtime he brought the day's *Times* with him, and over the course of three or four pints he completed the crossword. As I was rarely in at those hours I could never corroborate Chris's account of Ian being as 'silent as the grave' while he did the crossword. The only words he spoke were 'Good day' when entering and leaving, and 'The usual please,' when asking for a pint of mixed.

In the evenings it was a different matter. Ian would sit the far side of the fireplace from Bob, quietly but determinedly discussing issues of the day with whoever was prepared to listen. Like Bob, he was something of a monologist, but his talk was full of pith and moment. He was, in fact, a man of considerable learning, who years earlier had been a technician and demonstrator in the University's physics department. Drink had cost him his livelihood, though he was allowed to leave with a generous early pension and as a result had enough money in his pocket to pay for the upkeep of a modest terraced house on the local estate where he lived with his widowed mother, who no doubt cooked and cleaned for them both, as she did for 'Don, my kid brother,' which was the soubriquet Ian rather grandly bestowed on a younger version of himself, a merchant seaman, so Ian told us, who from time to time accompanied him to the Oak, bringing with him a chessboard he would spread out on a table before challenging anyone, 'anyone at all,' to a game.

Naturally, people were at first nervous of taking on someone who, for all anyone knew to the contrary, might be a grand master. Even after Don had lost an opening match or two with moves of startling ineptitude watchers-on remained suspicious. Suppose he suggested playing for money? We might then see an altogether different Don. He did make the suggestion, and some trepidatious soul rose to the challenge. As I remember, it took Don five moves, six at most, to lose his queen and declare himself beaten. And so on, as Swift more or less said of fleas' constancy, 'ad infinitum'. He never won a game, seemed to love every minute he played, and all the time he played, and lost, Ian watched over him with a benign smile. My beloved brother, he seemed to be saying, in whom I am well pleased.

Ian himself never played, though from time to time he would tell stories of classic encounters between chess masters of old as well as of the present. Kasparov versus Fischer was a specialty, an epic tale of East versus West, a Cold War encounter between two mavericks which Ian narrated with compelling gravity. And there were others. Ian told all these stories well, and while he spoke you could see that Arthur Crouch, listening enthralled, was sufficiently diverted from his role as faithful retainer to the glowering egotist on the other side of the fireplace to attend solely to Ian's words. It was not unknown for him to express his appreciation by an involuntary 'Oh, aye,' at which point Bob might mutter to the wallpaper, 'That's all *you* know.'

But it wasn't all Ian knew, far from it. The Saloon Bar being no larger than the front room of an average size family house, he could listen in on most conversations. Intercessions were frequent and might range from 'I think you'll find that the record Hutton overtook was Bradman's three hundred and thirty-four,' to 'Could I suggest that you may be referring to *Madame* Curie?' or 'I rather think Cook's last voyage was probably rather earlier than the nineteenth-century, may I suggest you could be confusing him with Franklin?' or 'Might Byron, rather than Binyon, be the poet you have in mind?'

These intercessions were always made with a decent show of hesitancy and most of the Oak's regulars admired Ian as well as being slightly in awe of him. A few, though, were irritated, even resentful. Bob was of course *primus inter pares* among these, though to my surprise Chris was not far behind. The landlord's resentment became so keen that on one occasion he decided to challenge his innocent tormentor. On Chilwell High Road – to all intents and purposes a continuation of Beeston's High Street – was a junk shop, *Boden's*. Boden – George to all – specialised in house clearances and his shop was crammed with furniture and household items, including piles of books, some still in their dust-jackets, others, the majority, scattered about in various degrees of dilapidation. I often rummaged through these and invariably came away with goodies.

Though an excellent judge of furniture and hangings, for which he charged what he always referred to as 'competitive' prices,

George knew nothing about books, nor did they interest him. Accordingly, he priced them by weight. A brick-heavy manual on car maintenance might cost you two quid. An uncut first edition of poems by James Stephens (52 pp) which I one day unearthed from beneath a pile of cushions cost me a few pence. I even came by a complete, twenty-six volume *Enclyclopaedia Britannica* (1911 edition), for three pounds. Intended for India, it was printed on very thin (rice) paper, but even so … I am, or anyway was, a pretty good poker face when it comes to disputing the marked-up price of books in antiquarian shops, but on this occasion I was so amazed/startled by George's asking price that in disbelief I blurted out *Three Pounds?* 'You get the case as well,' George said, defensively.

I may have reported this find to Chris, though if so I can't remember. But I *do* remember that early one evening, when I'd called in to buy a pack of the small, cheap and not very nice cigarillos I then smoked, he asked me whether I could get him an encyclopaedia from Boden's. 'A single-volume one,' he said. 'Nothing pricey.'

No problem on that score, I told him, though I'd no idea whether George would have in stock what Chris wanted. Fortunately, he did, and for ten bob I was able to supply the landlord with a battered copy of *The New Standard Encyclopaedia and World Atlas* (Odhams n.d.) But why did he want it?

'Shut Ian's mouth,' he said, 'That's what I'm after.'

It was early evening and soon enough, and following Bob's appearance, Ian arrived on cue, bade us good evening, asked for his usual pint of mixed and, having received it, took it into the Saloon Bar.

I hovered, watching from the passage as Chris, having flicked through the encyclopaedia's pages until he found an entry that had him nodding, and, with the light of battle now in his eye, marched into the bar where Ian, pint in hand, was settling himself.

'Right, Ian,' Chris said, 'You're so bloody clever, so answer this. When did James the Second go into exile. Exact date, please.'

Ian didn't miss a beat. 'Well,' he said, 'it all depends whether you're going by the Julian or Gregorian calendar.'

Chris gawped at him for several seconds. Then he left the room. 'Bloody books,' was all he said as he retreated behind the bar and threw the encyclopaedia into a corner. 'Bloody waste of time.'

6: Star-Gazing

One evening, Ian sold me a telescope. As Harold's business showed, the Oak was a place of transactions, some of them pretty dodgy, but Ian's sale had nothing in common with, say, my agreement to buy from Bob his daughter's hockey bag. 'Just the thing for your cricket gear,' Bob had told me one Sunday lunchtime, when I came in lugging my holdall and bat, off to play against Ilkeston Tradesemen. 'Room for your bat as well as all your clothes.'

I bought it – in most senses of that phrase – sight unseen, for thirty bob, and when he arrived with it the following evening I could see at a glance there was barely space for a pair of socks and a shirt, let alone the rest of my kit. I was told that afterward he enjoyed telling Arthur how he'd taken me for a ride. 'Money for old rope.'

'Oh, aye,' Arthur said.

The telescope wasn't old rope, but nor was it at all what I had in mind when I offered to buy it, again sight unseen. That evening Ian and I were talking about astronomy. Or rather, Ian talked while I listened to his enthusiastic account of the astronomer Herschel, whom he counted among the great, and of whose work, especially in building his own telescope, he'd made a study, which included the all-important contribution of Herschel's sister, without whose researches, Ian said, he doubted Herschel could have succeeded. (Many years later, when I read Richard Holmes's splendid *The Age of Wonder,* that fascinating account of various Enlightenment scientists, I realised how accurate Ian's estimate of her significance was.) Ian told me that he himself had been so fired up by what he learnt of Herschel's labours that he decided he'd try to build his own six-inch telescope. It took him several months, working all his spare hours, – grinding the lenses accurately was a particularly tricky business -- but in the end he succeeded. Sadly, however, the results were disappointing. 'Trouble is, the night skies over the Midlands are hardly ever clear,' Ian explained. 'If it's not industrial pollution it's the amount of artificial light from street lamps and the rest.'

I knew what he meant by an excess of artificial light – now called light pollution. The first time I became aware of what city lights could do to the night sky was when I was in Edinburgh at the beginning of the nineteen-sixties. Some years earlier, when I'd often been in night-time London, wandering the streets or moving between pubs and jazz venues, I became aware of how much brighter the city lights were from those soon-doused evening lamps of the suburbs, how dazzling, how thrilling. But I was at street level and it never occurred to me to think about how far the light rose into the night sky. And Reading, where I spent years as a student before becoming a young lecturer, was at the time no more than a small market town, and seemed to go to sleep well before midnight.

But in nineteen sixty-one I was directing a student production of Pirandello's *Lazarus* at Edinburgh's Festival Fringe, and while there I lodged some way up one of the city's hills. The first evening I came out onto the doorstep of the house where I was lodging, gazed, astounded, down on the city, on the blaze of yellow and pink dazzling up into the night sky, and my first, panicky thought was that the Bomb had been dropped and the whole of Edinburgh must be on fire. Such a response tells you how deeply scared many of us then were about the possibility of nuclear war. It also of course tells you that for most of us light pollution was a new and as yet unnamed phenomenon.

Three years later, by now married, I arrived with Pauline and our two-year-old son in Nottingham, and was shocked by the intensity and spread of the industrial smog that burdened the city. I can remember going into a second-hand bookshop soon after our arrival and handling a book, soot from which imprinted itself on all my fingers. The next year, the clean-air Act was passed and gradually the city's air began to clear and the high number of respiratory illnesses decrease; but that took a long time. So I could believe Ian's story that he'd never been able to make much use of his lovingly constructed six-inch telescope. A combination of light pollution and industrial smog had prevented him from seeing the night sky with any clarity, and after a couple of years he'd dismantled it.

Where was it now, I wondered? In the outside lavatory of his house, I was told. Odd. Why put a six-inch telescope there? I'd expected Ian to say it was in a cupboard or perhaps chucked in the back of a kitchen drawer. How much would he want for it? I'd just been paid some royalties for a book about Dickens, and fancied standing on the back lawn, telescope clamped to my eye as I peered up at the heavens, searching out the Great Bear or The Plough, or one of the many constellations whose names, some of which I'd learned at school, had gone from memory, though now they would be visible to my eagle eye as I stared at new worlds. After all, a six-inch telescope might well be three times that length when extended.

Ian diffidently suggested twenty pounds, mentioning that grinding the lenses had been a tricky business.

'Done,' I said, and in exchange for his promise to bring the telescope the following evening, handed over the money. 'Might be an idea to bring your car,' Ian said, 'it's heavy, and awkward to carry.'

Heavy? A six-inch telescope? Did I look *that* weedy?

'I'll bring a bag,' I said.

'Suit yourself,' Ian said, and next evening he arrived on the dot with the telescope.

Or rather, he came into the Saloon Bar and told me that he and the telescope had been delivered by taxi, and that the cab was waiting outside the street door. 'I could do with some help in getting it all out,' Ian said.

I went with him. And then I understood.

On the pavement was a large wooden box, propped beside it a round, lattice-work metal tube, getting on for a foot wide and some six feet long, and beyond that a set of steel rods resting on a heavy-looking square metal base. Ian paid the driver and I looked inside the box. A pile of inch-thick, as it seemed, transparent dinner plates stared up at me.

'Those are the lenses,' Ian said. 'Twelve in all, though you don't need to use more than four at a time, chosen for the atmospheric condition. You *do* need to take care slotting them in, get the order right, make sure they're correctly adjusted, though before all that you have to put the base into position, set up the support structure' – motioning to the rods – 'so that it holds the body and allows you to raise and lower the telescope as you want.'

He watched as I tried to lift the box containing the lenses. 'Did you bring your car?'

'I'll run and get it,' I said.

It took us most of the evening to get the telescope set up, by which time I was too exhausted to try it out. So we left it, glimmering between our garden's two apple trees like a ghostly howitzer, and returned to the Oak, where we arrived just in time for a final drink.

'Ian,' I said, as we raised our glasses to mission accomplished, 'do you mind telling me, what exactly *is* a six-inch telescope?'

'What you've now got,' Ian said. Then, as I shook my head in puzzled wonderment, he explained. 'Six-inch lens, it means. They take a lot of grinding, as I may have mentioned.'

'You did,' I said, 'and thank you.'

7: How Chris Came to the Oak.

One Saturday lunchtime, a few weeks after the installation of the telescope I went into the pub for an early pint before heading off for that afternoon's cricket. As he drew my mixed, Chris, who since my purchase of Ian's telescope had taken to calling me Galileo, asked genially, 'Found any new planets, by chance, any UFOs, any army of little green men sliding down a moonbeam???'

'I can't even locate a chimney pot,' I said. It was more or less true. Trying to align the lenses so as to gain any clarity of vision was proving a problem. 'Still, it looks good as garden furniture.'

Chris laughed obligingly. 'Want any more?' he asked.

'Any more what?'

'Garden furniture.' And in answer to my puzzled expression, he said, 'There's a table out back that'll soon be going begging.'

'Oh?' But I was still puzzled.

'A few more months and Margaret and I will be leaving,' Chris said. 'Time, gentlemen, please. I'll be sixty-five, retirement age. The brewery will want me off the premises.'

I was startled, no, shocked. I'd assumed that he owned the pub, but no, he was a tenant, and now Shipstone's would be installing a new occupant. I was so used to seeing Chris behind the bar, occasionally helped by trim, middle-aged Margaret, that it had never occurred to me that one evening I might open the street door and see a stranger waiting at the end of the passage to serve me. It wasn't a prospect I relished.

And what of Chris, how did he feel about the prospect of retirement? 'How will you cope?' I asked him. How would *we,* his regular clientele, cope, was really what I meant. Chris was a well-liked publican. Affable, tolerant of the pub's often eccentric habitués, though capable of exerting authority on the rare occasions when someone who'd drunk too much had to be shown the door. And he kept his ales in excellent condition. The Oak's range was strictly limited – draught beer, bottled ales, whisky, rum, gin, a few bottles of all-purpose wine – that was about the stretch of the alcohol he served, but all of it done with dispatch.

I only once saw him lose his poise. That was when a friend of mine brought into the pub a new girlfriend, a Home Counties twinset kind of person called Perdita.

Chris asked her what she'd drink. 'Sherry,' she said.

'*Sherry?*' Chris's voice became something between squawk and screech. After a moment, he pulled himself together. 'Red or brown?' he asked.

Perdita turned to my friend, bewildered. Were these Midland terms, variations on what folk in Surbiton knew as dry or sweet or what ….?

'Amontillado, perhaps?' she suggested.

Chris gawped, helpless.

'Have you got a dry sherry?' my friend asked.

Chris retreated to the back of the bar, where Margaret was filling in some forms.

There followed urgent conversation, and a minute later Margaret emerged with an empty bottle in her hand, exited through the street door, and by means of a side window I saw her running down the lane. She was heading for the grocer's shop on the corner which sold cooking sherry from the barrel.

Chris, once more master of his fate, came back to where the three of us waited. 'Your drink will be with you immediately,' he told Perdita. He smiled ingratiatingly but still couldn't trust himself to utter the word 'sherry.'

Now, as I drank my pint, I said 'Well, Chris, I'll miss you, and so will we all.' Which was, I knew, the truth, although Big Bob would probably deny it.

Chris thanked me. 'I'll not miss the early mornings and the late nights,' he said, 'but I've enjoyed my years here, I'll say that. Anyway, we'll not be far off.' And he told me that he and Margaret had been able to buy a bungalow in nearby Bramcote, large enough to house them both as well as their daughter, Lesley. 'Though she'll be off soon enough, I guess.'

I guessed so, too. Lesley was a vividly attractive, lithe teenager, soon to leave school, after which she planned to go to Art College somewhere in the North. My great friend Barry Cole, then at the peak of his success as poet and novelist, who would often come up from London for the weekend, and other times besides, enjoyed flirting with her.

On one occasion Lesley, who happened to be in the Saloon Bar that evening, a Thursday, asked him what he did for a living, 'seeing that you don't seem to have a regular job.'

'I'm a writer,' Barry said, rather grandly.

But if he hoped to impress her, he was in for a shock. 'Writer!' she said with some disdain. 'How boring.' Then, 'What do you find to talk about?'

Slightly nettled, Barry asked, 'What do *you* like to talk about?'

'Horse-riding,' Lesley said. Whether true or not, and I doubt it was, her reply did for Barry.

Had Chris always been a publican, I wondered. He laughed. 'Pure chance,' he said, and, the hour being still pre-noon and there being as yet no other custom, he gave me a barebones account of his early years.

He'd been born in nineteen hundred and eight, in Farnham, Surrey, where his father was a small builder. 'Peter Christmas, he named me after him.' Ah, so Chris wasn't short for Christopher? No, Chris said, and moreover Christmas was a rare enough name for most of those bearing it to come together for an annual meeting and dinner, usually in London though other cities might occasionally be chosen. For example, when he himself was fifteen, the dinner was held in Southampton. 'My father took my mother and me, not for the dinner itself, mind, but so we could all stay in a hotel for the night. Decided my future, that did.'

Because that evening, Chris and his mother, free to wander about town, inevitably paid a visit to the waterfront and saw, from a distance, one or two of the vast liners in dock 'Massive. Took my breath away, I can tell you. Floating hotels, I know they're called, but to me they were more mysterious than that. Hotels stay where they're built but a big ship goes off, sails across the world.

I mean one evening you're in Southampton and a week later you're in New York. Can't do that in a hotel.'

At the age of fifteen Chris had already left school. His father wanted him to join the business, 'But I didn't fancy it. Life on the ocean waves, now, that was different.'

'Bartender?'

Chris laughed. 'Never gave it a thought. Anyway, I was too young. But there had to be jobs on a big boat I could try for. Of course, my folk were against it so I bided my time, did some hod carrying for the old man, but I wanted to get away, I knew that much.' The problem, Chris said, was just suppose he got to Southampton, what then?

A mate of Chris's came up with an answer. Billy Hastings and he had already started to earn a few shekels performing a song and dance act they'd put together and with which they toured local pubs and any places that would have them – church functions, hospitals, social evenings for various clubs: whatever chances came their way. They weren't bad, either. Not Mickey Rooney and Judy Garland, exactly, but they got more cheers than boos. Billy had learnt tap dancing as a small boy, Chris owned a ukulele he'd bought with money his father tipped in his direction, taught himself a few chords – a few were all you needed – and although they were under-age and so couldn't enter pubs, 'out back' was different. 'Out back' was where many public houses had rooms separate from the bars and which could be hired for dances, amateur dramatics, jumble sales, you name it. The two of them gradually came to be regulars at these events, given ten-minute spots – *Bill and Coo* they called themselves – and after a year or so their fame (ho, ho) spread to surrounding towns and villages and they were able to ask for a proper fee.

That was when they decided to make a break for it. Billy had talked with a friend just back from the States who'd told them that you could work your passage on a big boat by providing entertainment for paying voyagers. Not first-class, mind. These had society orchestras to play for their nightly dinner dances. But second-class, steerage ... no problem. This friend, who was a contortionist, might be vague about the details, but according to him, or so Billy reported, all you needed to do was to get yourself to Southampton, ask around at the shipping line offices, and if something didn't at first come your way you could do a bit of street busking. Cinema queues – they paid well. Then, if you played your cards right – put on a good show – someone would hire you for boat work, proper pay, time ashore in New York or wherever, might even land a contract on Broadway ….

'Wet behind the ears, both of us,' Chris said. 'But when you're young you want to see the world. We never even thought about passports, or anything else. Just pack up and let's get going.'

A few weeks later, after scraping together enough money for train tickets to get them to Southampton and leave a few coins in their pockets for a night or two's dossing, they were there.

'And then off to the New World?'

Chris laughed, shook his head. 'Never even left Southampton,' he said. And in a very few sentences, uttered between serving customers who were by now beginning to arrive in numbers for their lunchtime beers, he explained that a quick tour of the offices made plain that Billy's mate must have been having them on – no passports, no work permits, not even identification papers, no thank you. So they went to a pub, got permission to 'play out back' and by the end of the evening had been hired to do their act on a nightly basis. 'For a week, see how it goes.'

They were still there, by now on reasonable money, and with food and lodging above the pub thrown in, plus extra from taking the mug round – 'usually filled with copper and a few bits of silver' – when news of the Wall Street Crash reached them. 'After that, dreams of a new life in America were out the window.'

'So you stayed in Southampton?'

Chris nodded but he was now too busy behind the bar to say more. Anyway, it was time I was on my way.

But as I put my glass down and headed for the street door, he called after me, 'Don't forget about the table.'

'I won't, promise,' I told him and a few days later, when I dropped in, he found time to take me up the yard at the back of the pub to inspect it.

The pub's back yard had at one time housed a long covered section which formed the skittle alley. The other side was the

'Gents', or, as it was commonly called, 'Pissing Alley', also with a corrugated roof. Now that skittles had fallen out of favour in most Nottingham pubs, the Oak's back yard had become a storehouse for empty crates and cardboard boxes, broken furniture, an old mangle, and, half-hidden beneath piles of old rags, the table. It was a recognisable pub table, right enough. The thick, scrubbed wood top was about three feet long by a foot wide and was supported on wrought-iron legs. A handsome-looking object.

'How much?'

Chris proposed a couple of quid and I said 'Done.' Then we went back inside.

I had to get a friend to help me carry it home from Villa Street, across the main road out of town, then up the twitchel past the local primary school which Ben and Emma attended and so to our house, a quarter of a mile at most, but, given the weight of the wrought-iron legs alone, a severe strain on arms and backs. Still, we managed it and now, getting on for fifty years later, the table, wooden top rotten but legs as good as ever, remains in our garden, as does the telescope's six foot long casing, poking up through bushes and wonder to all who do the same espy. I never did get the damned thing to work properly and eventually offered the box of lenses to Harold.

'And what would I do with them?' he asked.

'Not sure,' I said, 'dinner plates, perhaps? Anyway, I thought in your line of business it was the rule never to look a gift horse in the mouth.'

'There's an exception to every rule,' Harold said.

8: Mine Host

In the months before Chris pulled his last pint at the Oak he found the time to tell me a good many stories about his earlier life. It was as though, having bought the table, I'd established myself as someone to whom he could entrust memories of the young Peter Christmas. Over those months I listened to a good many tales about his days as an 'entertainer', and of the offers he and his mate Billy had been made to turn professional.

'I thought you *were* professional,' I said. 'You told me you got paid.' But I suppose they were really 'semi-pro', a term much used in the jazz world for those who take care to keep the day job.

'We did alright,' Chris said. 'Made enough to get by. Never signed any contracts, though. It was always cash in hand, ask no questions. It was how it worked in those days. But blokes used to hang around the places where we performed, keen to sign us up. One in particular. A real Mister Ten Percent, he was. "All legal and above board. Trust me, I'm an agent." He called himself Larry Fiddler, can you believe? Wore bow tie and spats, reckoned he could get us into stage shows, variety halls, even the radio. "Just sign here and I'll see you get on in the business. I've handled big names in my time."' Chris laughed derisively. 'We asked him to name one. A bit of humming and ha-ing before he mentioned Leslie Sarony.'

'Who?'

'Quite,' Chris said, 'though to be fair Sarony did have his successes in the 'thirties. A few songs, like, "When the Guards are on Parade". Ever heard of it?' And when I shook my head, Chris said, 'Well, he wasn't a headliner, but that was the best our man could come up with.' So, 'No thanks,' we said, 'we'll manage ourselves.' Another laugh. 'And we did, for the best part of a couple of years. But then Billy left me, went off to London, said he'd been made an offer by a cousin to join him in running a cocktail bar. And that was that, never heard from him again.'

'You didn't try to find another partner?'

Chris shook his head. 'Didn't try. To be honest, I'd had enough. Billy was right, not that he said so, but we were never going to get anywhere in that world. Besides, we'd both got bored of the same old routines, night after night, and I'd met someone, fancied a better life.'

'Margaret?'

'No,' Chris said, 'Margaret came later, and then he was off to attend to his bar duties so I had to wait for a future occasion before hearing more.'

It came the following Saturday. Like most pubs, the Oak opened early on Saturday evenings, five-thirty, when the first drinkers came in, waiting for deliveries of *The Football Pink* to arrive by van at the street door. *The Pink* was a phenomenon. Given the speed at which it was printed at the *Nottingham Post* offices and made ready for distribution, it was a surprisingly professional production, six pages of reports and results, and adjustment of the league tables, all of them recorded from the moment the referee blew his final whistle, or so it seemed. Men waited in the passage for the arrival of the Oak's supply to thump against the door, someone would run to collect it and bring it to the bar, Chris would cut the binding tape, and then, as the waiting throng paid for their pints and a copy of the *Pink*, it was out with their football coupons, *Littlewoods* or *Vernons*, and check the results. I don't remember ever hearing that anyone at the Oak made a killing on the pools, though from time to time there'd be a modest victory, and in anticipation of scooping the trough, pints all round would follow.

The Four Aways was a favourite with many Oak veterans. It paid out less well but you stood more chance of landing a prize, or so the soothsayers in the Public Bar believed, though judging from the mixture or curses and cries of exasperation that rent the six o'clock air, such belief was ill-founded. Either Wigan Athletic had done the impossible and held out against mightier opposition, or bloody Arsenal had fiddled themselves a draw by means of a late penalty – 'got the sodding referee in their pocket' – or …. Well, there was always one team or another which had done the entirely unexpected and defied the certain opinion of every pundit in the land.

Among the pundits was Tommy Lawton. A former England international and Notts County centre-forward, Lawton remained a local hero long after his playing days came to an end, many of which had in fact been spent at other clubs. He lived in a council house somewhere in the city and on more than one occasion was taken to court for failure to keep up with his rent or for raiding his gas meter in an effort to pay off outstanding bills.

These offences were reported in the city's *Post*, often as front-page news, but did nothing to dent his image. In fact the *Post* employed him to offer 'expert' opinion on the current Forest and County teams, and though the opinion never amounted to more than a few clichés along the lines of 'Forest have got a chance if they play their best,' or 'County can be guaranteed to try,' they were greeted with grave nods of approval by local fans.

And why not. Lawton *was* a great footballer, and like all footballers of his generation, including the best, he was treated appallingly by club owners and management. I remember reading about how in 1947, Wilf Mannion, another England international whose career, like Lawton's, was interrupted by the war, scored twice for his country in a match against 'All Europe' held at Scotland's Hampden Park, and had then to return home by train in a crowded third-class compartment, standing all the way, while various footballing bigwigs sat drinking whisky in a first-class compartment. After his career ended he became a labourer, had to sell his medals, and died destitute.

I once saw Mannion, a golden-haired dazzler, play. My father took me as a ten-year-old to Highbury to watch a game between Arsenal and Middlesbrough. Among the Middlesbrough side were George Hardwick, then captain of England, and Jimmy Gordon, later to be bucket-and-sponge man at Brian Clough's Forest. After the game, my father, who during the war had played in the Army team alongside both Mannion and Gordon, took me down to the away team dressing room to meet them. Too over-awed to speak, I remember the occasion chiefly because they gave me signed photographs of themselves, which, many years later, I passed on to my grandson. By then footballers were not merely stars of the back pages, many of them were millionaires. Not so Lawton. But I never heard anyone in the Oak so much as tut-tut over his misdemeanours.

***

As I came up Villa Street one Friday in late summer, not long before the date of Chris and Margaret's departure, I saw a Shipstone's van outside the pub. At first I thought the van might be acting as a removal vehicle for the landlord's goods and chattels, but the double trap doors beside the pub's front were open and I could see a drayman manouevring a large barrel into position so as to roll it down the wooden slope into the deep cellar directly beneath. 'Evening, Chris,' I called out, hearing his voice shouting instructions, and he called up, 'Give us a hand, will you.'

I went in. The door down to the cellar, beside the bar, was propped open, so, following instructions, I went down the brick steps and for half-an-hour in that cool place helped Chris uncouple empty barrels from the pipes and push them up the slope to where the assistant drayman stood. Then, with the head drayman helping out, we got the new barrels down, raised them into position on chocks, Chris took a mallet and bashed in the plugs so in order connect the pipes, and then my part was done. I looked around at the pipework, the racked-up barrels, the crates of ale neatly stacked, the trestles on which smaller barrels stood, the whole complicated but orderly arrangement, and for the first time appreciated why complimenting a landlord on his being 'a good cellar man' wasn't empty praise. As a swan glides gracefully over water while underneath its webbed feet paddle furiously, so ....

Upstairs, the draymen and I stood at the bar watching Chris work the beer handles as the water that gushed out gradually turned to beer.

'The last time I'll be doing this,' Chris said. An experimental pint was pulled, held up to the light, found to be without floating impurities, handed round, sipped, the head drayman announced

'All clear,' and they and I were given pints while Chris contented himself with a modest half which, as usual, he scarcely touched.

After the draymen had gone, I asked Chris how he had come to learn his trade. By the early nineteen-seventies the biggest breweries in the land – especially Watney's, Ind Coope, and Whitbread – were going around the country buying out small breweries together with as many independent pubs as they could, then turning them into ghastly 'Ye Olde Worlde' pretences of days of yore (unspecified). Tenants were disappearing and were being replaced by managers, tame victims of the men with clipboards who drove around England in Ford Mondeos and spoke of profit margins and customer satisfaction and product. As for the product itself, the beer these places had to sell, Watney's Red Barrel, Ind Coope's Double Diamond, Whitbread's Tankard, were identidrink: gaseous, metallic, uniformly *horrible*. Liquid solder, as a friend of mine remarked.

But the worst of this was as yet to come. Chris's beer was, as the same friend claimed, 'ambrosial paradise'. A shade hyperbolic, perhaps, but it really was excellent. No doubt all casks left the Shipstone maltings in fine condition, but not all landlords looked after their supply. There were several Shippos pubs I knew of where the beer was, as one disgruntled toper somewhat obscurely alleged, like washing-up water after a tinkers' wedding. It's sometimes struck me that the terms of opprobrium beer drinkers create for ale of which they disapprove is far more inventive than those used by wine-tasters to account for vintages to which they give the thumbs up. I love Thurber's piss-take: 'It's a naive little domestic Burgundy, but I think you'll be amused by its presumption'. But beer, though permitting what in the eighteenth century Lord Kames called periphrasis ('as when we improve upon the word "sky" by calling it "the blue vault of heaven"'), doesn't encourage such pretentiousness. It must be something in the water.

Anyway, on the occasion when I helped Chris rack up those new barrels of beer, he told me that after he'd hung up his tap shoes he began to take a serious interest in the pub business, learnt what he called 'the tricks of the trade', and by the end of the 'thirties he'd acquired the tenancy of a pub in a village not far from

Amesbury. But then came the war. He volunteered for service, failed his medical because of poor eyesight and was given work with the catering corps. As a result he was sent to the Chilwell army depot, which was where he met Margaret, who was spending the war years 'stuffing powder into bombs,' as he put it. 'Dangerous work, that was,' Chris said. 'There'd been a massive explosion in the earlier war, killed over two hundred of what some locals still called the "Canary Girls". They were given that name because of the sulphur they'd had to work with.

But no such problem for Margaret. The place didn't go up in smoke and Margaret didn't turn yellow.'

There was a moment's silence before he next spoke. 'So after the war we got married. Best move I ever made.' He laughed but I sensed the depth of his emotion.

'And did you try to go back south?'

'Margaret wanted to stay here. She's a Nottingham girl. And you know what they say about Nottingham girls?'

I did, but couldn't imagine he was referring to the legend that the city's women were free with their sexual favours.

'They prefer Nottingham men,' he said. 'So I knew I'd have to stay.'

He applied for and landed the tenancy of the Oak and they'd been here ever since. 'So now you know.'

'And you'll have seen some changes,' I said in an old codger's manner. 'Down Your Way.'

'The Snug most of all,' Chris said, taking me seriously.

'That little room where Margaret does her sewing?'

'That's the one.'

The room in question, beyond the Saloon and facing across the passage to the bar itself, was where Adam Frith had interviewed Harold and me the morning after Sheffield Tommy's killing. I couldn't imagine how a room so small, and so unremarkable, could have seen many changes. Drinkers making their way along the passage as they headed for the outside toilets would call out a greeting to Margaret if she was in there, but although someone might pause in the doorway to exchange a few words, as I myself did, there was scarcely the room to step inside for a chat. Margaret's sewing machine, basket of washing, ironing board and clothes horse took up virtually all the space.

And yet, Chris now told me, the Snug had once been an important room in the Oak. Really? Oh, yes. Really. Every Saturday lunchtime it had been the agreed meeting place for men released from their working week in the lace factory opposite. They met in the Snug to celebrate their freedom by piling into the room and there consuming oysters and Guinness, well, pints of mild, because the Oak didn't run to Guinness. '*And* they were dressed for the occasion,' Chris said, 'it was part of the ritual. Proper suits, black bow ties and bowler hats. Exceptions not permitted.'

And where did the oysters come from?

'Grimsby,' Chris said. 'Brought across by the morning special. Grimsby Docks to Nottingham – not much more than an hour and a half. And from there straight to Nottingham pubs and restaurants, in and out of the city. Not just oysters, either, various shellfish – mussels, cockles, alive, alive, oh. You must have seen the sellers going their rounds.'

I had, I realised. On Friday and Saturday evenings these men, in white coats and straw boaters, would make their way from pub to pub, ringing handbells as they went, baskets on their arms and calling out their shellfish wares. In the early nineteen-seventies, these came ready packaged, but in the immediate postwar years they were sold still fresh in their shells, and the baskets in which they were heaped held small saucers on which the shells could be stood. 'Small forks, too,' Chris said. 'A bit of a palaver that was, gathering everything up when they'd done. Still, it was good business.'

'I can believe it,' I said. 'There must have been barrel loads of oysters coming across from Grimsby.' Because I'd also noticed the various pubs and restaurants across Nottingham that advertised themselves as oyster bars and restaurants. There was, for example, the rather grand Akins Oyster Bar on the Mansfield Road, and there was, too, King's Oyster Rooms, a basement bar below Yates's Wine Lodge, both venues distinguished by their black and white marble floors, similar to those you saw in high-class fish sellers.

'But you don't have oysters on the menu,' I said to Chris.

'No', Chris said, smiling sadly, 'crisps and pickled eggs, that's about the extent of it nowadays.' The oysters, he explained, finished some years back, at about the time the lace factory shut its doors for the last time; and though a few sellers still toted other shellfish around Nottingham pubs on Friday nights, the trade was drying up. There were fewer vendors, and thanks to Beeching the cross-country trains were less frequent; in fact many of the lines out to the smaller sea-ports had gone. 'I told you I'd seen some changes in my time here.'

'So the Snug has gone the way of all flesh. A shame. It amazes me, though, that you could ever get more than three or four grown men in there.'

For answer Chris came out from behind the bar and steered me across the passage to what I thought of as Margaret's sewing room. We edged our way inside and he pointed to a framed photograph on the inner wall. 'There you are,' he said. 'Proof.'

The photograph, some two feet by one, showed a group of men standing shoulder to shoulder. They were in dark suits, bow ties and bowler hats, oysters in one hand, pint glasses held aloft in the other, all of them smiling obligingly at the camera. 'Taken about twenty years ago, that was,' Chris said.

I studied the photograph. Behind the men I could make out a window set in a brick wall I was pretty sure belonged to the lace factory. 'That's not the Snug,' I said.

'They took it in turns,' Chris said, deadpan, 'The oysters were laid on this,' rapping his knuckles on what I thought of as his wife's sewing table. 'When you'd got your supply you collected your pint of mild and mingled, or on sunny days you could stand in the street if you wanted. Good occasions they were. Very sociable.'

I looked again. I recognised several of the faces, two in particular. 'That's Harold,' I said, pointing to a stocky man in the back row, 'and that's Arthur Crouch. They didn't work in the factory, did they?'

'But they were partial to an oyster or two,' Chris said.

'And what about Big Bob? I don't see him here.'

'Wouldn't have let him join in,' Chris said. 'I'd have had a riot on my hands. Anyway, I expect he grew his own.'

Part Two: Derek and Edie

1: New Faces

The news that Chris would be giving up the tenancy of the Oak, which he'd held for twenty-five years, soon got about. A shame, it was widely agreed, he'd been a good landlord. We'd miss him, miss Margaret, too. Someone organised a whip-round to which most of the pub's regulars contributed – even Bob parted with five shillings – and with the proceeds we bought a carriage clock for them to take into retirement, and had it inscribed: *For Chris and Margaret from all regulars at the Royal Oak.* No need for anything flowery, someone said.

On their last evening, a Friday, the two of them announced they would throw a party, to be held from six to eight o'clock. Speeches were made, the clock was presented, we sang 'For they are Jolly Good Fellows', Margaret and Lesley, home from her art college, circulated with cold fried sausages and slices of pork pie, pints were pulled, and the healths of the landlord and family were toasted. Then the pub was open for business as usual.

Pauline and I, having shaken their hands and wished them well for their retirement, left early, as many if not most did. A few went on to neighbourhood pubs for a final drink of the evening, others, the majority, preferred to make their way home. I suspect we all felt, as I certainly did, that to drink elsewhere that evening would have seemed wrong, an act of disrespect.

The Royal Oak was shut for the weekend, to give time for Chris and Margaret to move out and the new tenants to move in. Beyond being told that their names were Derek and Edie and that they'd be coming up from Basingstoke, we knew nothing about them.

The following Monday morning, as I was about to step into the post office, I was hailed from the other side of the street by an older man I recognised as a Public Bar habitué, though I never knew his name. He was one of those Chris used to dub 'The Hospital queue'. They comprised several semi-invalids who at the beginning of each week presented themselves at one or other of the local medical centres to get signed off from work for the coming seven days, after which they'd throw away their crutches, so to speak, and hurry to the Oak in time for opening hour.

'I'm on my way to try the new landlord's beer,' he called. 'See if he knows how to look after it. He's got a hard act to follow.'

'Good luck,' I called back, but declined an invitation to join him. 'It's only ten o'clock,' I shouted, 'you'll have an hour's wait.'

I didn't explain that I'd be working at home that morning, finishing a book I'd promised to deliver to my publisher by the end of the year. I'd once used that excuse to a regular I'd met in the High Street and been up-ended by his reply. 'How long's it take to read a bloody book? Any road, you can do it when the pub's shut.'

So it wasn't until Saturday lunchtime that I found time to call in to the Oak, and when I did so I was in for a surprise.

Both Public Bar and Lounge were crowded, as was the passage, and among the regulars were many faces entirely new to me or which I recognised as belonging to Beestonians I sometimes passed in the street though I'd never seen them in the Oak. Why were they here?

The answer, I soon realised, was that some had come out of curiosity, others because, so Ian, who now joined me, hinted, they wanted to see whether, having been previously shown the door by Chris for rowdy or otherwise unacceptable behaviour, they'd be welcomed back by the new tenants, and still others hung around because the Oak might now be a place to do business that Chris wouldn't have permitted. These last included petty criminals, wide boys and, as the old jazz standard had it, card dealers, card sharpers, and those with an Ace in the Hole. I didn't of course know that then, but over the coming weeks, Arthur Crouch, who seemed to know them all, would put me wise to their various activities, their ways of turning a penny. And the names he gave them, or by which they preferred to be known, suggested that the Oak had suddenly turned into Beeston's version of Damon Runyan's New York underworld: of Angie the Ox, Rusty Charlie, Society Max, Feet Samuels, Harry the Horse, all those Guys who inhabited Mindy's Restaurant.

But on that Saturday I stayed only long enough to introduce myself to the new tenants, drink a pint of mixed – excellent – and ask out of politeness how they were settling in. Edie, who had served me, stocky, in blue jumper and grey skirt, her frizzy hair outlining a round face which from time to time would break into a wide smile, remarked that so far she had no complaints except for the weather.

'Parky is what she means,' Derek said, as he came to stand beside her. He was slightly built, bespectacled and with a wandering left eye, dressed in check shirt and yellow pullover.

Even those few words made audible his accent, broad Hampshire, familiar to me and countless thousands from John Arlott's BBC cricket commentaries. I couldn't stop myself from asking whether by any chance he followed cricket? He laughed, shook his head. 'Don't like anything much beyond an occasional game of shove ha'penny,' he said.

'You'll be alright here, then,' I told him. Shove ha'penny was played on a regular basis in the Public Bar.

'If I ever get a chance to sit down,' Derek said. 'We've both been on our feet since the moment we arrived.'

Then he was called away to fill the glasses of several newcomers and I downed my drink and, having offered my best wishes for their future here, I left.

As I stood in the doorway, Harold arrived. 'You'll have to shout your order,' I told him, 'the place is heaving.'

'It's been like that all week,' he said. 'Give it a few more days, I would, and then it'll settle down. Most on 'em will be making tracks for their regular watering holes.'

'Where have this lot come from then? I've not seen many of them before. Have they been bussed in from the city?'

'The Commercial or Cricks, more like,' Harold said. 'Foreign territory, the Oak is. They're giving it a go.'

The Commercial Inn, a Mansfield pub, tall, gauntly handsome, stood some two hundred yards away, on the main road out of

Beeston. The newer, unattractive, sandstone Cricketers was nearer still, at the top of Villa Street. As with the Oak, both had served as hostelries for workers from the local lace factories. But Beeston drinkers were a territorial lot. It took a great deal to make them move of their own free will from one pub to another. Harold, who had lived in Beeston all his life and knew far more about its ways than I could ever hope to, was no doubt right. The newcomers would soon be gone.

2: Painting the Oak White

A couple of weeks after Derek and Edie's arrival, the Oak had reverted to normal. Or had it? Not all the newcomers disappeared. And among those who chose to remain were some who brought with them a new atmosphere. Not edgier, exactly, but certainly racier, the kind of men you might expect to find at racecourses. They *were* all men, middle-aged, and they kept to themselves. They stood in the passage, greeting each other, but scarcely bothering to nod to us, and few if any of them chose to sit at tables in either bar. They weren't any better dressed than the pub's standard clientele, but you felt that their style of dress was intended as a kind of declaration, though what that might be wasn't at first apparent. Open-necked shirts, dark jackets and trousers, no boiler suits or overalls, no whiff of the shop floor about them. When they paid for drinks I noticed they didn't bother to count whatever change was tipped into their open palms. They took for granted that they'd been correctly charged, that nobody would risk taking liberties with *them*.

They came in the evenings, and at Saturday lunchtimes, and how they dressed wasn't dependent on the day of the week. When any of them spoke to Bob – and they all seemed to know him – he gave them bare, and I sensed, reluctant recognition. It was as though they knew who was in charge, and it wasn't him.

Would they have been welcomed by Chris? It seemed unlikely. Anyway, under his tenancy the Oak wouldn't have appealed to them. They brought with them a hint of the underworld, of being on the wrong side of the law. Still, even in Chris's time there were almost certainly a few among the regulars who were shady dealers, though they were frank about it. One I'd discovered by accident. Soon after our arrival in Beeston I'd gone into the Oak to buy a bottle of stout, explaining to Chris that I was in a hurry because

I'd promised Pauline to finish seeding a patch of earth in the back garden that had under previous owners been used for growing vegetables – 'a wartime garden' – but which I'd promised our two small children to grass over so that it could provide a play area for them and their newly acquired friends.

'You'd be better turfing it over,' a man standing in the passage beside me said. 'Put turf down and after a week you'll have a lawn fit for the kiddies and their mates to tumble all over. He was Irish, someone I scarcely knew. I laughed, said something to the effect that I had no knowledge of how to come by any turf, and that anyway Pauline had already bought some seed.

'Let's have your address,' he said, 'I know a man who'll be able to see you right. Cash in hand, mind, he can't be doing with any other form of payment.' He held out his hand, winked. 'Pat's the name,' he said.

Without really thinking – I was in a hurry – I took his hand, which was enormous, felt mine squeezed in a powerful grip, gave him my address, left the Oak, and spent the evening seeding and watering the square of earth that was intended to become a lawn.

Two days later, in the early hours of the morning, I was woken from sleep by a loud banging on the front door. In a daze I went downstairs, dragged open the front door in the expectation of having to turn away someone in desperate need of the Methodist Minister, and there, on my doorstep, stood the Irishman.

'I've your turfs for you,' he said, 'waiting in a van. Show us where they're to go.'

In pyjamas and bare feet I took him round to the back of the house. He flashed a torch over the raked patch of garden, said, 'Give us half an hour,' and half an hour later knocked on the back door. 'All done and dusted,' he said. 'Thirty pounds in cash. You can pay me this evening.' And was gone.

I went back to bed.

Later that morning, I looked out of the kitchen window, expecting to see a stack of turfs waiting to be unrolled over the patch of bare earth where the children, who'd run outside, would be standing. Not a bit of it. There was no such patch. Instead, the two of them stood in the middle of a grassy lawn.

'It's magic,' they said as I went to join them.

That evening, when I handed over thirty pounds, I wondered aloud where the turfs had come from.

'A young feller I know,' the Irishman said, unblinking.

'Otherwise known as Chilwell golf course, if you ask me,' someone said to whom I later recounted the story.

As for the Irishman, I saw him a few more times at the Oak and we always nodded, even smiled our mutual recognition. But that was as far as it went, and by the time Derek and Edie arrived he'd long gone.

The new landlords weren't in any way to blame for the petty criminals who now began to use the pub. I don't know exactly how and why the crims came to be at the Oak. No doubt they felt the need to move on from wherever they'd previously met to talk, make deals, arrange some 'job' or other. For them, the fascination of the new was no doubt that it kept them one step ahead of the Law. New venue, new landlord. Just what was needed.

I'd already encountered this process when, rather more than a decade earlier, a friend and I, about to embark on postgraduate work at Reading University, he as a physicist, I in literary studies, found a flat we could share above a newly created coffee bar on the edge of town. *The Café Olé*, it was called, and it advertised itself as selling 'Interesting Contental Sandwiches.' (The sign-writer was either deficient in what Bertie Wooster might have called the Spelling Department or was simply short of paint – or space.)

As soon as Carl and I moved into the flat above the café, the owner, a cheerful Scot, suggested that one or other of us might like to make a bit of cash by acting as the café's occasional manager. This would leave him free to run his dance hall somewhere else in town. We'd have little to do, so he promised. Sell the occasional 'contental' sandwich, work the coffee machine – he demonstrated how to use the brand-new Gaggia – take the money for bottled soft drinks, and provide loose change for those wanting to feed the juke box. (Favourite records included Billy Eckstein and Sarah Vaughan singing 'Passing Strangers' and Ella Fitzgerald, 'Manhattan' and 'Every Time We Say Goodbye'.) Closing time ten-thirty, all out by ten forty-five. OK? he asked. Carl thought he'd rather not. But, OK, I said.

The café was intended for students and those of a similar age. Before long it was taken over by a gang led by a thug known as Charlie the King of the Teds, whose nightly arrival at the café was wonderfully choreographed, a thing of comic beauty. Precisely at ten-thirty each evening, as the café was about to close, a chauffeured black Humber Snipe would glide to a stop outside the door. Having emerged from behind the wheel, the driver, in dark glasses, would walk round the car, open the rear door, then step onto the pavement and fling wide the door to the café. As he did so, Charlie would ease his black-suited bulk from the car's back seat, camel-hair coat draped across his shoulders, dark glasses clamped onto his face, and make his entrance.

He would peer about him, point to a table, and wait for it to be cleared for him while the chauffeur, by now at the counter, placed his order. 'Black coffee, no sugar.'

Having spoken, the chauffeur then stood beside the designated table, and, having lit a cigarette for Charlie, would remain silently standing, while Charlie took sips of coffee and gazed indifferently about him. 'I could buy this place several times over,' his gaze suggested.

At approximately eleven o'clock, the chauffeur would saunter to the café door and Charlie, having taken care to drop his cigarette butt into his cup, usually still half-full, would stand, slowly exit, and slowly fold himself into the back of the Snipe. Having shut Charlie in, the chauffeur would go to the driver's seat and slowly, slowly, the car would be eased into the Reading night. Naturally the café door was left wide open.

After several nights of this unvarying performance, I decided to act. Next door to the café was a pub called The Turk's Head where I occasionally drank and where, when I did so, I encountered at the darts board a vast Irishman called, would you believe, Mick. Mick was an expert at darts, so accomplished, indeed, that he scorned feathered darts. Instead, he played, and invariably won, with especially sharpened six-inch nails. Would

Mick, I enquired, be willing for an inducement to sit at the door of the café each evening at ten-thirty? The inducement was free coffee and sandwiches, in exchange for which Mick would deny entrance to someone I was keen to bar from the café. Was this acceptable? It was.

The following evening at ten twenty-five, Mick installed himself near the door while a plate of ham sandwiches and a large cup of coffee were placed before him. A few minutes later the Snipe arrived, the door opened, and the chauffeur entered, followed by Charlie the King of the Teds.

I nodded to Mick, who rose from his seat as Charlie was about to accommodate himself at a nearby table.

Mick tapped Charlie on the shoulder. 'Out,' he said.

Charlie took one look at Mick's bulk, knew when he was on a loser, and left.

It wasn't though the last we heard of him. A week or so later we read in the local newspaper of Charlie's appearance in court on a charge of assaulting a police officer in Reading's town centre.

Charlie's defence was that he approached the officer and, intending to ask the time, tapped him on the shoulder, whereby to his surprise the officer fell into the gutter.

Sentence. Six months custody in Oxford City Gaol.

The café was now free territory for Charlie's hangers-on or, of course, rivals. First up was Ken Spicer. Ken, Unlike Charlie, was by and large a peaceable man who became besotted with an art student called Nancy. Nancy regularly took her evening coffee in the *Olé*. One evening Ken arrived at the café with a bolt of cloth which he had liberated from a large draper's in town and which he wished to offer Nancy as proof of his undying devotion. Unhappily for Ken, he was followed in by two policemen and in due course Ken followed Charlie into Oxford gaol.

Then came Chick, who wore a black leather jacket, had a very broken nose, and wished to be known as 'The Hardest Man in Berkshire'. He was, however, soon supplanted by 'Bill the Blade', who carried a small knife in his belt and brought with him a posse of mini-thugs whose abiding concern was the form of the dogs they followed at the local race track.

None of these posed a threat to the café's management. They sat together, kept their voices low, and seldom bought anything more than a coffee.

They were, I think, friendly with 'Cookie', so called because she ran the kitchen where lunchtime meals could be bought by the unwary, though I heard that she was better-known for performing abortions at her back-street premises where she also provided 'upstairs rooms' on an hourly basis. Mrs Gamp could have taken her correspondence course.

Edie belonged to an entirely different world. She was someone I became very fond of, a woman of sturdy character with very definite ideas as to how to fulfil her role as Derek's partner. She occasionally took a turn behind the bar, but was more often to be met accompanying their two small children, a well-turned-out boy and girl, to and from the local nursery school, or shopping on the high street, or standing at the rear of the bar while she prepared food for what she advertised as 'Business Lunches'.

Not business as in three-course meals with napery, wine glasses, and fruity laughter. What Edie had in mind were a series of variations on chips and …. sausage, egg, ham, or fish. (Meaning pre-fried in breadcrumbs.) And, for those who favoured the possibility of a second course, there was a choice of cheese and biscuits or ice cream.

The idea for these lunches had come to her, she told me, when she discovered that the local council offices had recently moved to within hailing distance of the Oak. All these men and women keeping office hours. They'd fancy a decent lunch.

She was right. Within a month of the new tenants' arrival, Edie installed a superior oven in the kitchen behind the bar, turned the Snug into a store with freezer unit and plate racks; and within a week of announcing Business Lunches the Lounge Bar was serving up to two dozen people each working day. No Fancy Dan accoutrements, though a few tables were allotted slim vases with everlasting flowers to go with the salt and pepper; but the food was fresh, served piping hot, and, as at least one of those eating at the Oak was wont to observe, 'There's no beating a pint of Shippos and a plate of sausage and chips.'

That particular complimentarian, a decent enough man, worked in the same office as someone I came to loathe, a braggart whose name, I learned was Fricker, and who for all that he made great play of being married, dominated conversation with talk of the women he had taken to bed or whom he had marked down as future conquests.

Like the rest, he wore a two-piece suit with collar and tie, and they more or less filled the Saloon Bar between one and two o'clock. Anyone in need of the more usual pint and bag of crisps took to standing in the passage or joining the drinkers in the Public Bar, most of whom were workers from the local factories, although one or two of the hospital queue lingered over their near-empty glasses.

***

Edie was full of plans to improve the Oak. Not long after she began her weekday lunches, she decided to smarten up both bars. 'They need re-decorating,' she said, her expression making clear that it was going to happen whatever the regulars thought. My guess would have been that the regular topers wouldn't much mind what she planned. As long as the beer tasted good – and under Derek's watch there was no chance it would deteriorate from the standard Chris had set – I don't suppose anyone noticed what colour the walls were presently painted.

What colour was that anyway? From countless years of cigarette and pipe smoke, a tawny yellow seemed to predominate, though above the spot where Bob sat the ceiling had long since turned mahogany.

'I want white all over,' Edie said. 'Then I can put some pictures on the walls. Brighten the place up.'

'The woman's touch,' someone suggested, leering, and was silenced by Edie's rejoinder. 'I can't imagine the woman who'd want to touch you,' she said.

And when was this re-decoration to happen, and how? Derek and she had a pub to run, after all, bars to keep open morning and evening. Or did they plan to close for a few days?

Edie explained her plan. The work would be done over the coming weekend. Saturday morning the Public Bar would be shut while undercoats were applied to walls and ceiling, woodwork ditto. All drinks would therefore be served in the Saloon. Afternoon and early part of the evening Saloon given undercoat. Both bars open in evening, standing room only. Sunday morning, Saloon shut for topcoat and oilpaint on wood. Afternoon and early evening, reverse. Monday morning, for all able to lend a hand, passageway. Ditto, the following morning. All done and dusted by Tuesday evening.

Edie had planned it with the precision of a military exercise. 'But won't you have to pay extra to painters and decorators for weekend work?' I asked.

'I shan't be paying anything,' Edie said, smiling. 'Free food and drink, of course. I'm relying on volunteer help.' She would, she announced, be drawing up a rota, which would be pinned above the bar the next evening. That would allow time for adjustments. 'Anyone who can't manage one shift can change places with someone who can.'

'Oh,' I said, meeting her steady smile. 'Alright, put me down for two stints.'

'I already have,' Edie said.

The following Saturday morning I turned up for my shift. I was in good spirits. I'd driven a hard bargain with Edie who'd accepted my request that in return for an extra shift I'd be given the trophy I craved. It was already installed in my study, where I'd taken it the previous evening, having prised it free from the fireplace wall in the Saloon Bar where it had stood, at a guess, for the best part of the Oak's existence. Edie was quite happy to see the back of it, she said, especially as she had a picture in mind to cover the empty space.

My prize, or reward, or trophy, was a plaster bas-relief, some two and a half feet square, of a galleon in full sail steering toward the viewer, on its billowing foresail a large red-painted Maltese cross, between that and the mainmast a tall black funnel from which smoke corkscrewed, while from the open gun-ports, where you might have expected cannon to poke out, there were three banks of oars. It was a wonderfully absurd amalgam of trireme, galleon, and steamship, and I never saw its like in any other Shipstone's pub. It occurred to me that its maker might have been inspired by the three stanzas of 'Ships', Masefield's breezy celebration of different ages of shipping, a poem which generations of schoolchildren had learnt by heart, and so created a tongue-in-cheek tribute to Shipstone's beers. I loved it.

3: Bill and Ted

My fellow painter that Saturday morning was a man I knew as Hedgehog Bill. I'd learnt this from my friend, Bill Cole, a jazz musician who from time to time sat in with the group I was then playing cornet with, The Ken Eatch Jazzmen. Bill Cole, who by the time I came to know him, also lived in Beeston and who drank in all the town's pubs, was a fascinating man. A bass-player who, like most bass-players in the jazz world, could puff away on tuba in street marching bands – he was also a more than passable rhythm guitarist – Bill had been on the road for a number of years with the Ken Colyer Jazzmen, at that time probably the best exponents of New Orleans style in the UK. On a gig in Nottingham he had met and fallen for the daughter of the University Professor of English Language, a dear man called Ken Cameron. Sue introduced Bill to her father and Prof Ken was happy to greet Bill as a prospective son-in-law.

There was however one difficulty. In fact, there were two. Bill was already married, and though he and his wife had lived apart for most of their married life, he would have to buy himself out of his marriage. And, as Bill 'lacked the necessary lettuce', to use the memorable words with which Sky Masterson's father explained to his son that *he* was broke, Professor Cameron agreed to pay for the divorce settlement. Then there was the question of where the couple were to live. Sue didn't fancy the vagaries of life on the road, and anyway she was training to be a teacher. Bill therefore offered to put down roots in Nottingham. Furthermore, he decided to give up most, if not all, touring. But how then to earn a steady income?

Again, Ken came to the rescue. He sensed that although Bill had done with formal education at an early age, he was a man of great native wit, as he himself was. Ken came from a working-class family in Blackburn, and had gone to university after returning from a distinguished wartime career in Bomber Command. Through a mixture of hard work and sheer intelligence, he had risen to be a senior academic and much-admired historian of Place Names, and he was always keen to assist others who came from his kind of background. Accordingly, he helped Bill gain a place on a teachers training course, and in due course Bill was appointed to teach history at what was almost certainly Nottingham's toughest inner-city comprehensive. He throve there, was adored by those he taught – in this his musical prowess undoubtedly helped – and was widely admired as a first-class as well as knowledgeable teacher.

I discovered for myself how highly Bill's students regarded him when, years later, I acted as external examiner for a PhD student at Sussex University. The candidate was a young man who had produced an outstanding thesis on working-class fiction, and after the viva ended and talk had become general I asked him where he came from. Nottingham, he said. Which School? He told me. It was the school where Bill was still teaching. 'Did you come across Bill Cole?' I asked him. 'My favourite teacher,' he said. 'An inspiration to me and to a good many others.'

And then he told me a story which I love. One day in the early eighties – I think it must have been at the time I was spending a year in Greece which was why I was then unaware of it – the school where Bill taught was briefly in the national news. There had been a fight outside the school gates during which one boy was knifed and died of his wounds. Naturally the gutter press was at once onto the story, and the following day several journalists and, I think, a TV crew turned up outside the school's front gates. Teachers watching from the staff room were appalled. The school already had a reputational problem over discipline and the last thing it needed was more adverse publicity. Dinner hour was about to begin and the waiting press would be hovering, ready to interview whichever pupils they could get hold of. What to do?

Enter Bill Cole. Or rather, exit Bill Cole from the school's main door. At the front gates he confronted the posse of journalists eager to interview any pupils or members of staff they could buttonhole. What followed can't be known for sure, or rather how Bill by fair means or foul got them to back off. But there is general agreement that within a very few minutes the gentlemen of the press began to slink away, perhaps intimidated by the sheer power of Bill's personality, as well as the deep, volcanic power of his voice. It must have helped, though, that two squad cars were soon on the scene. These had been summoned by Bill before he left the school buildings, and their prompt arrival no doubt owed something to the fact that a local inspector played jazz clarinet with a group Bill occasionally helped out.

There was doubtless a degree of embellishment in the story I was told, the more so when you consider that Bill, for all his bulk, was rather less than five feet tall. Not that he saw this as a disadvantage. Far from it. He was, he often enough remarked, one of the few bass players in the history of jazz who never suffered from a bad back.

He also told me on an occasion he came to the Oak for a drink, that Hedgehog Bill, who happened to be in the pub that evening, was so named less because of his wild, spiky hair, than because in dry weather he preferred sleeping under hedges to being tucked up indoors. 'Bit like me,' Bill added. 'When Sue's away I'll often roll up in a dry ditch.'

'Really.'

'I'm two-fifths gipsy that's why. And old Hedgehog, he's got gipsy blood in him.'

Most of us took for granted that the true explanation for Bill's nights in a ditch was that after a late-night gig he'd arrive home full of ale after Sue had gone to bed and, not wanting to lose a night's sleep, she'd simply locked him out. Sue was a devoted wife, but still, a girl can't go on laughing all the time.

I don't think Hedgehog was much of a drinker. In fact after we'd finished our morning stint of painting the parlour, he accepted only a large mug of tea and a cheese sandwich. He and I worked in what might be called companionable silence for a good three hours, and soon after midday we'd completed our shift. And as Arthur Crouch had more or less completed his allotted task of applying an undercoat to the woodwork, we all felt we deserved a break. Edie agreed. Work had gone to plan: she was a happy woman.

Walking home I found myself wondering about Hedgehog Bill. What exactly did he do for a living? And what brought him to the Oak – and many an evening he was, I knew, in the Public Bar or standing in the passage. I didn't think that a love of beer could be the explanation for his presence. Nor did he seem in need of conversation. His few, monosyllabic, utterances were not those of a man eager for the cut and thrust of public house discussion. The Hedgehog was no wiseacre. It came to me indeed that he was rather like Captain Cuttle's friend, Bunsby, whom Cuttle, that warm-hearted man, held in high regard and whose intellect he delighted in praising. 'You carry a weight of mind, easy, as would sink one my tonnage soon,' he tells him. Cuttle is determined to read into Bunsby's silence evidence of a perspicacity which would strike most as plain stupidity.

So how did Hedgehog Bill get by? Was he a snapper up of unconsidered trifles? Did he live by his wits? Unlikely. Or was he in possession of craft skills I was unaware of. His work with the paint brush didn't suggest so. Clumsy doggedness was nearer the mark. And though he removed his old, baggy jacket before starting work, he took no care to protect his equally old, raggedy sweater and brown corduroy trousers from numerous smears of paint. They were the clothes he always wore. And when he peered at you through his smeared spectacles, one arm of which was held to the frame by wire, there wasn't much to suggest a light burning within. I'd have to ask Bill Cole. He'd know.

***

By Sunday evening all except for the passage was done. There would be no celebratory party that night, however. The new curtains had not yet been hung nor had Edie found time to arrange on the walls pictures she claimed would brighten the Saloon. These tasks would be undertaken at odd moments during the forthcoming week and a grand opening was to be arranged for the following Saturday lunchtime. Drinks on the house for all who had contributed to the re-painting and decorating. And by popular request, no speeches. Dress, as usual.

I was busy all that week and so it wasn't until Saturday that I could see for myself the pub in its new splendour. There was something of a carnival atmosphere about the Oak that morning. Word must have got around because the pub was packed, and, the weather being fine, people stood outside, in the narrow street, or on the opposite curb, while pints of beer were passed along the dazzlingly-white passageway and over heads to those who couldn't get in.

I forced myself through to the bar to be greeted by a triumphant Edie who, in the middle of pulling pints as she worked beside Derek, was accepting congratulations from all who came within hailing distance. She looked flushed and happy, almost as though she was a bride. And it has to be said that in her green silk dress, a white carnation tucked behind her left ear, her appearance did suggest a new status. Landlady of the Royal Oak at Beeston. Creator of her domain. A virtual coronation.

The only person looking less than happy was Bob. He'd arrived at an early hour in order to make sure of his corner seat, and there he sat, silent and glowering. I was told that on entering he had taken a look around before delivering himself of the opinion that with white paint everywhere 'the bloody place looked more like a hospital than a pub,' and that in reply Derek had told him that if a hospital was what he was after it could easily be arranged.

Laughter from most. From Bob, silence.

Later that lunchtime, as the crowd began to thin, I found myself in conversation with a regular of the Public Bar, one of those who'd wielded a brush for Edie, and who answered to the name of Ted. Or was he called Ted because he *was* a Ted, the last one in captivity, so to speak? I'd seen him around Beeston often enough, invariably leading a whippet, cigarette in the corner of his mouth, usually in dark glasses, and like Hedgehog Bill always in the same dress, though his was very different. Bill's clothes hung off him, almost as though he hadn't finished dressing, whereas Ted took great care over his appearance. Black suit, with drainpipe trousers, long drape jacket and black velvet lapels, white ruffled shirt and bootlace tie, vast mutton-chop whiskers that made it look as if a pair of ear phones had slipped down his face, oiled hair carefully coiffured in the style known as DA (District Attorney in barbers' adverts, otherwise Duck's Arse), and black suede boots with excessively thick crepe soles. 'Brothel creepers', such boots had been called when I was a schoolboy, and they belonged with Teddy Boy outfits of the kind which Beeston Ted espoused and of which he was surely the last exemplar.

Seeing Ted as he padded about town in his brothel creepers reminded me of an occasion my mother told me about, when she and my father had been to the West End to see the great Tony Hancock in a variety show. In one sketch Hancock prowled the stage dressed as a Teddy Boy until he suddenly stopped and confronted his audience, an anguished expression on his face. 'Cor,' he said, 'these crepe soles don't half draw your feet.'

As we stood now pressed shoulder to shoulder in the passage, I was momentarily tempted to ask Beeston's Ted whether, as I had heard, brothel creepers caused foot rot. But I had another question to put to him. As part of the improvements to the Oak, Edie had installed a juke box in the Public Bar, and I gathered that Ted's opinion had been sought as to what music might find favour with the regulars. The juke box was playing but the hubbub was too great for me to make out who or what was on.

'Elvis?' I asked Ted. 'Nah,' he said, 'Ruby Murray. I love her. She used to own a pub at Sandiacre.' A later inspection of the playlist revealed that among other vocalists Ted featured on the juke box were Doris Day ('Secret Love'), Dickie Valentine ('Mr Sandman') and Dean Martin ('Wine Drinker').

Ted was in fact a gentle person. In the days before we came to be on speaking terms, I once sat behind him on a bus taking us both to town when a woman carrying a large shopping bag clambered aboard and, recognising Ted, plumped herself down beside him.

'Not seen you for a good few weeks,' she said. 'You been off on your travels?'

Yes, Ted agreed, he'd been doing a job down south.

'Expect you're glad to be back among your own kind.'

Ted said nothing.

There was a pause, before she next spoke. 'How's that daughter of yours goin' on,' she asked him. 'She still livin' with that homosexual feller?'

Ted nodded.

'Funny business, that,' the woman said.

'He makes lovely porridge,' Ted told her.

'Still,' the woman said, her voice hinting at troubled respectability, 'it's not the kind of thing you expect on Central Avenue.'

Central Avenue was the street that cut through Beeston's council estate, from which quite a few of the Oak's regulars came, though not, I think, Ted. At all events, I'd often seen him going into or coming out of a trim little house nearer to the pub. And I see him still, though his abundant and carefully coiffured hair is now white, as are his mutton chops, and he rides around Beeston on a kind of four-wheeled electric bike featuring handlebars at least as wide as a Harley Davidson's.

4: Raising the Tone

During our Saturday morning's stint as decorators, I'd suggested to Arthur and Hedgehog Bill that we ought to act like professionals.

'What, join the union?' Arthur asked. 'I'm a union man already. Can't join another bleddy union, can't afford the dues for one thing. Anyway, it's not allowed. If you did a proper bleddy job you'd know that.' And he laughed round his cigarette in genial contempt.

'I mean sign for our work,' I said.

I was remembering that while a university student, I'd worked during one summer break for a small building company in outer London, where I'd witnessed the firm's painter and decorator sign his name on each wall that he was due to paper over. 'Why are you doing that?' I'd asked and been told that proper craftsmen always found somewhere to place their signature. 'Always have, always will. Why not? They've done the work.'

Later, I'd read Ruskin's praise of Gothic craftsmen for, as it were, providing evidence of their freedom, their individuality, in decorating architectural work with tokens of their skill. Gargoyles, grotesque embossments, misericordia, and the like. And Pauline told me that her father, having made a stone seat in his garden once, had cut his initials into the underside of the seat.

I mentioned this to Arthur, who said, reasonably enough, 'Don't see how we can do anything like that, not when we're whitewashing. Any ideas, Bill?' The Hedgehog's silent shrug suggested he hadn't, so in the end Arthur and I painted our initials on the underside of the bay window's sill.

That moment came back to me when, years afterward I read in a now defunct local newspaper the obituary of someone called George Stewart. 'Born in Newcastle-upon-Tyne,' the obituarist begins, 'George was brought up in children's homes in the north of England, never knowing who his real family was,' and goes on to remark that 'although he never married or had his own family, he was much liked and respected as gardener and handyman.' Moreover, George 'had an enquiring mind and his opinion was sought on various issues, and he always left his signature on walls before papering.' The obituary lodged in my mind and I wrote a poem, 'As a Rule', which was published in my collection, *Things to Say,* prompted by the obituary's praise for a man who might seem entirely anonymous, but who left something behind, some assertion of identity.

I was here, I am here, I will be here. How wonderful, how moving, that a man who came from nothing, who was quite without family, should nevertheless more than survive the odds stacked against him of being a *good* human being, a responsible citizen, should be a man with qualities, and should find the means, however modest, to announce his presence on earth. *Ecce!*

***

Now that the pub was newly painted, now that it served lunchtime food, now that I had obligingly taken away the bas-relief above the Saloon fireplace, Edie was keen for the bar to acquire additional *cachet* by displaying pictures on two of the walls. Accordingly she went into Nottingham and spent some time in an 'Art Gallery – Furnishings for your Home' – from where she returned by taxi, bringing with her two framed works which she at once hung in the 'Lounge', as she preferred the Saloon bar to be called. Above the fireplace she positioned one of those reproductions of the painting known as 'The Green Lady', very popular in public places, especially bars and restaurants, during the nineteen-seventies. Semi-naked, liquid-eyed, with long, glossy tresses, the Oak's exotic lady met the indifferent gaze of Bob, of Arthur, and of such other regulars as bothered to look in her direction. And on the opposite wall was an island featuring a sandy beach overhung by palm trees, at the water's edge an unpersoned rowing-sized boat with fishing nets draped across it, and in the distance, a haze of mountain tops. *Tropical Paradise,* the picture was called.

Having now raised the tone of the Lounge Bar, Edie announced herself well satisfied. And the room, with its heavy, navy blue curtains, and sea-green carpet, did look very different, so we all agreed. But over the coming weeks the 'Island' picture underwent a peculiar metamorphosis.

I think it was Geoff Dyer who wrote that once you've bought and hung a picture you tend after a very short time to cease paying it any notice. Whether any of the regulars in the Lounge Bar of the Oak noticed what was happening to Edie's picture I can't be sure, but I do know that *nobody* commented on the changes.

I first became aware of a subtle alteration some weeks after the picture was hung. I was in the Lounge for an early evening beer when, happening to glance at the *Tropical Paradise*, I noticed a large fly sitting above one of the palm trees. It looked bizarre, that fly, outlined against the garish sunset, and I reached out to flick it away. The fly did not move. I flicked again. Still no movement. I went closer, peered at the insect and saw that what I'd taken to be a fly was in fact a flying saucer, and that this one, presumably executed in black biro, and scarcely more than a quarter of an inch in size, came complete with undercarriage, wheels dangling from struts rather than, as I'd supposed, a fly's legs. It was a most accomplished miniature.

A week later brought another flying saucer, this one hovering over the far-off mountains. A further week and there were two more, barely distinguishable against the darkening sky, and then, in a brazenly transformative move, a whole squadron of them came homing in over the trees in the middle distance.

And *still* nobody noticed. Who was doing it? Who was desecrating Edie's picture? Who was the phantom artist? Should I alert her as to what was happening in the Lounge?

Before I could decide, matters were taken out of my hands. One evening, rather more than a month later, by which time the skies above the tropical paradise had become thick with alien objects, I went into the Lounge and found that 'Paradise' had been replaced by another painting, this time of a sturdy, full-leaved oak tree. The painting was behind glass.

I never felt I could ask Edie about her lost paradise. Nor was there much point in discussing the matter with any of the regulars though I did once ask Arthur Crouch what he thought of the tree, pointing to the oak as I put the question.

Arthur peered at the painting and shrugged. 'Once you've seen one bleddy tree, you've seen 'em all,' he said. Did he then prefer the painting that had previously hung on the wall?

'What painting?'

'The *Tropical Paradise*,' I said.

'Don't remember,' he said, half apologetically. Then, rallying, 'Anyway, once you've seen one bleddy paradise you've seen 'em all.'

5: The Hedgehog and the Daimler

The Oak was a regular meeting place for several of my friends. Some were lecturers at the University who lived in and around Beeston, others were cricketers who fancied a drink after a match at our home – University – ground, or Labour Party stalwarts planning for council elections, or writer friends from the city or visiting; and then there was the occasional jazz musician who used the pub as a drop-off or pick-up point for those needing a lift to some out of Nottingham gig. Bill Cole would often ask me to take him and his bass when we were playing together at a venue where he daren't drive himself in his battered old Ford estate. Any late-night traffic policeman in search of an easy target who spotted Bill would know that he'd almost certainly be over the limit. Pull him over, issue a ticket, and be on target for the award of Mr Plod, the Pride of the Force. That, anyway, was how Bill saw it, and it didn't matter that he'd taught himself to drive straight when with drink taken. That itself was cause for suspicion. 'Step out of the car, please.' On more than one occasion when so invited Bill had responded by opening the car door and falling at the traffic cop's feet. So, at least, rumour had it.

Which was why, one evening, I agreed to take both of us to a gig at Matlock. We met according to plan. A pint for Bill, a glass of water for me, and then we'd be off. We were standing in the passage – no time to settle into the Lounge – when the street door opened and in came Hedgehog Bill. 'Can't stop,' he said to his namesake rather than to me, and, with unusual eloquence added, 'got a job on. Just need some fag papers.'

He bought the papers, turned to go, and as he did so the street door once more opened and in came one of my university friends, a social sciences lecturer. He held the door for the Hedgehog who nodded an acknowledgement but left without saying a word, and Bill and I, too, prepared to leave, Bill retrieving his bass from the

Lounge where he'd leant it against the wall, while I apologised to my friend for not being able to join him in a beer.

'That man who just left,' he said. 'Do you know him?'

'The Hedgehog? Bill knows him,' I said. 'Why?'

'Just wondered. I've seen him around at all hours, never seems to be in the same place twice. And what's he do for a living, I wonder.'

'He's alright,' Bill said as he reappeared. 'Freelance. Looks after people's cars, mostly.'

And we left.

On the road to Matlock, Bill gave me further information about the Hedgehog, though what he had to say didn't amount to much more than that Hedgehog Bill was someone who didn't believe in regular, nine to five work. Instead, he got by as an odd-job man, chiefly by putting in hours for a couple of local garage owners. 'Checking tyre pressures, oil, windscreen wipers, that kind of thing. A bit of a grease monkey.'

I repeated this information to my friend the next time I saw him.

'So he's a car mechanic.'

'I don't know about that,' I said. I wasn't at all sure how much Hedgehog knew about the insides of cars.

A few days later we were walking home from the campus when my friend remarked, 'That car mechanic friend of yours, I met him in the Oak a couple of evenings ago. Nice man, though not much to say for himself. I've asked him if he'll do a job for me, cash in hand. He said yes.'

We were turning up Villa Street now. 'What sort of a job?' I asked him. 'I don't know that the Hedgehog's much of a car mechanic, not an expert at all events. Are you sure about this?'

The answer came with airy confidence. 'Oh, no doubt about that. I asked him questions, he gave the right answers. Job on.'

We took our pints into the Lounge where, as we sat in our accustomed window seat I was told that the work the Hedgehog had agreed to undertake – for fifty smackers – wasn't for my friend but for his professor, whom I'll call Richards. Professor Richards was the proud owner of a veteran car, a pre-war Daimler, which he greatly enjoyed driving up and down England, but which had recently shown signs of needing some expert attention. The brakes in particular were a problem, too slack, worryingly slow in responding to foot pressure.

'And you've asked the Hedgehog to give his expert opinion about what's needed.'

'More than that,' I was told. 'He's going to give it a full service, replace any worn parts, have it all ready, good as new, a week from now.'

'And how are Richards and the Hedgehog planning to meet?'

'All taken care of. I've arranged to join them here for a drink early tomorrow evening. Your friend Bill the mechanic will take the car over and spend a week tinkering with it, after which he'll be bringing it back to the Oak and Jim Richards will be fifty quid the poorer, plus any extras for replaced parts. But he'll be rich in satisfaction.'

'I hope so,' I said. 'And by the way, and to be clear, Hedgehog Bill isn't a friend of mine, I hardly know him, and I certainly don't know whether he's a trained car mechanic. Or *any* kind of mechanic, if it comes to that.'

But my doubts were waved away. 'I've met Bill's kind before,' I was assured. 'Short of words but when it comes to doing the work they're sound as a bell.'

I wasn't by any means re-assured, but my friend's confidence silenced me. And maybe he was right. I didn't, after all, know any ill of the Hedgehog. If there was something dodgy about him, Bill Cole would surely have told me. So I drank my beer and we turned to other subjects.

A week later, though, the pub was made fully aware of the Hedgehog's dodgy nature when two policemen came looking for him. I heard all this the following day. The Hedgehog hadn't been present when the cops called in at the Oak and in fact I never saw him again. But he'd made off with a tidy sum of money for work on Jim Richards' Daimler which he'd never done. 'Not so much as spat on it,' Harold reckoned. This became evident when Richards, taking his newly-restored car out for a spin, lost control of the steering wheel, found out the hard way that the brakes didn't work, and the car left the road and crashed into a brick wall. Fortunately, he wasn't going fast, so he did himself no serious injury. But the car was a write-off.

Police enquiries were perfunctory. Derek gave what help he could, which was precious little – no, he didn't know the Hedgehog's real name and no, he hadn't a clue where he lived (though rumour had it that for several nights Bill had made his bed in, or under, the Daimler), and though one or two of the regulars admitted that from time to time they'd exchanged the odd word with the Hedgehog – 'wasn't he that bloke who came and went without leaving a forwarding address?' – the cops, having learnt nothing useful, jotted down a few names and within half-an-hour were gone.

'We shan't be seeing them again,' Harold reckoned. 'A professor who tries to get work done on the cheap so as to avoid paying tax …. '

'So they'll not be back?'

'Doubt it,' Harold said.

'Unlike the Hedgehog,' someone suggested. 'He'll lie low for a while, then he'll be in for a pint.'

'Hibernating,' Ted remarked. There was some laughter. Heads nodded. Hedgehog Bill had survived worse setbacks.

'But won't the police have asked Derek to tip them the wink if the Hedgehog shows his face?'

'Oh, ah,' Arthur Crouch said as he waited to have his glass re-filled. 'But like as not he'll tell the bogger to scram before he picks up the phone. Same for all on us.'

And, drink now in hand, he went to re-join Bob, who as usual was pretending indifference to passage talk.

I glanced toward Derek who had been standing behind the bar listening to all of this conversation, and who now met my look.

'Didn't hear a word,' he said.

6: Everybody Loves Saturday Night

The longer Derek and Edie's tenancy went on, the more the Oak changed. It wasn't only that the pub became increasingly thronged, so that night after night an increasing number of people crammed into the passage and the Public and Lounge bars, with the result that if you weren't in by seven o'clock you'd be lucky to find a seat anywhere; but the nature of the clientele expanded. Old habitués stayed loyal; newer drinkers began to establish themselves and were absorbed into the atmosphere.

Hard to say what exactly that atmosphere was. I sometimes thought of Pope's praise of ordered variety, 'where, though all things differ, all agree.' But no, it wasn't that. If you consult any dictionary you will find that there are two principal definitions of the word 'atmosphere': 1) The air or climate in a particular place; 2) A general pervasive feeling or mood. Even under Chris and Margaret, the climate of the Oak was different from other pubs I've known. Really, it was a micro-climate, and when Derek and Edie were in charge it was not merely desirable, it came to feel somehow uniquely so. The pervasive feeling or mood was one of subdued excitement. As you pulled open the street door you felt – well, I felt – that I was entering a place of good cheer. There was nearly always a subdued hubbub of talk, of laughter, and, often enough, during a lull in the rising swell of local voices you'd hear Dean Martin, in his mellifluous, slightly decadent-seeming crooner's baritone, singing of the bar in California where he sat, 'little ole wine drinker me'.

Wine in the Oak? Hardly ever, though for those desperate enough there were bottles of all-purpose white or red, each with a musty, corked taste. But it was beer that was the pub's glory. Beer that was reliably clean-tasting, with that bitter note any good beer requires, mollified and enriched by the mild ale which, when added to the pale gold of the bitter itself, made for the 'mixed' which was the all-time favourite for most of us. And surely it tasted even better because of the company. When I was a small boy, I remember my mother listening to a radio programme called 'In Town Tonight'. It ran early evening every weekday, lasted, I think, for fifteen minutes, and was introduced by a voice uttering the words, 'Once again we stop the mighty roar of London's traffic to bring you some of the interesting people who are – [slight pause then, as it were with upper-case emphasis] – IN TOWN TONIGHT.'

Going into the Oak of an evening, I would adopt a plummy accent and announce, to myself or any companion I had with me, 'Once again we stop the mighty roar of Beeston's traffic to bring you some of the interesting people who will be IN THE OAK TONIGHT.'

Because there *were* interesting people within. It's a commonplace that drink loosens the tongue. Not always, of course. The more bottles of brown ale he downed, the more firmly Bob's tongue was nailed to the roof of his mouth. And there were others for whom drink lent them the gift of tongues that guaranteed incomprehensibility. Chief among these was a man called Dennis – I never knew his surname – who with his wife, Doreen, arrived in the pub at about seven o'clock each evening. I think they came straight from work, he from labouring, she from work as an office cleaner. They would stand shoulder to shoulder in the passage, up against the bar counter, at first drinking silently – pints of mixed for Dennis, and for Doreen, gin – but, as the evening wore on, drink released both of them into strange forms of expressivity. Dennis would begin to speak, though I doubt that anyone understood a word of what he was saying. Not that it mattered. If you felt you were the one being addressed, you had simply to agree with him and all was well. 'Oh shanser woo wont bickly tros.' 'Spot on, Dennis.' 'Wooolah hargloss.' 'Quite agree.' And Dennis, who had startlingly blue eyes, would smile at you, a happy man.

As for Doreen. After several gins she would offer for approval her imitation of Old Mother Riley, hauling up her black skirt over laddered tights and trotting from bar to bar as she let rip whoops and skirls. And at the end of the evening, by which time Dennis would be comatose, his mate, as thin as a stick insect, somehow found the strength to haul him out of the pub, wishing everyone 'Good night' as she went and promising to see them the next evening.

How on earth did they manage to down so much alcohol? Christmas was their apotheosis, their time of greatest glory. Edie, I think it was, had the notion of suggesting to regulars that from the beginning of October they should tip into a large cake tin a weekly amount of cash, recording as they did so how much they were depositing, so that, come Christmas, she could tot up the amount due to all contributors who would then be able to convert it into drink for the festive season. A good idea, most of us agreed, and we also agreed to place our orders with Edie who would get in what we had ordered. All drink was to be collected at lunchtime on Christmas Eve. I went at the appointed hour to collect the bottle of whisky I was owed, and learnt that Dennis and Doreen had already gone off with their dues: a bottle each of whisky, rum, and vodka.

'They were waiting outside when I opened up,' Derek told me. 'I'm guessing they were keen to make an early start.'

They made an early finish, too. Rumour had it that by early evening they were back in the Oak, having emptied the last of their bottles – vodka, I think.

***

There were a good many regulars at the Oak who could put in some plucky work with the elbow. But most attendees were also there for the talk, for what the Irish called *craik*. It's a word lacking in English, probably because it's largely absent from our culture. The OED includes 'crack – gossip, discuss the news', but without placing the word socially. *Where* do you discuss the news? Well, anywhere people meet, I suppose. But 'crack' belongs above all other places to pubs.

Or it did. But then, in the nineteen-eighties came the re-invention of pubs. City pubs especially were now to be 'vertical drinking experiences'. And with their arrival, the talk I think of as pub conversation – from international news to local scandal – began to disappear. So, too, did older drinkers who enjoyed a pint as they sat to talk or play table games. There were no longer such tables to sit round, merely narrow shelves surrounding fake pillars, barely enough on which to balance a pint glass, and as a way of putting the kybosh on talk there was loud, piped, music and shouted, mostly monosyllabic utterances. Drink was what you were there for, talk was ancillary, an optional extra. Hence the verticality. Who needed seats? Cram the bodies in, get drink 'down your neck' – that horrid expression or its equally horrid alternative 'neck a bottle' – and who gives a damn for talk.

I remember once, in the early sixties, going into a Scottish pub, in Leith, and finding that although there were quite a few male drinkers sitting at the bar, there was no talk. Each man sat on a high stool, chin in hands as his elbows protected his glass of beer and, in most cases, a chaser, staring uncommunicatively ahead. Taking my glass from the barkeeper I looked around for somewhere to sit. There was nowhere. Before I could comment, the barkeeper leant across to me. 'You hae your drink and you get oot o' my hoose,' he said.

No, I know that this is exceptional. I've had some great evenings in Scottish pubs, including an especially memorable occasion when, soon after my rebuff in Leith, I was in The Abbotsford in Rose Street where the poet Robert Garioch was holding court and toward the end of the evening he suddenly thrust a manuscript of his poems into my arms, telling me as he did so to look after it because he expected to be assassinated before morning. Next morning, hung over but glumly aware I should try to return his poems to the poet, I staggered off to The Abbotsford. An unfazed Garioch stood at the bar – perhaps he'd been there all night – and I gave him back his poems. He took them without, as I remember, thanking me, though he did suggest I buy him a drink.

'A tavern seat is the throne of felicity,' Johnson famously observed, and as famously entreated a friend, 'let us fold our knees and have out our chat.' 'Chat'? Hmm. It suggests inconsequential talk, trivial talk, talk of trivia. What men used to refer to condescendingly as women's talk. Even Cowper's 'Divine chit-chat' is linked to his association with a number of women friends. To Lady Throckmorton, Lady Austen and above all to his enduring friendship with Mary Unwin, 'My Mary'. A hint of the 'Blue-stocking' there, perhaps, not chatterboxes, but still …. Here is Johnson himself, in his Dictionary, on the verb 'To chat'. 'To prate; to talk idly; to prattle; to chatter; to cackle'. Not good. Ah, but then, 'to converse at ease'. Yes, that's it, *that's* what a pub atmosphere makes possible, what it encourages. Chairs around tables, settles pushed up against a wall, banquettes. You sit and you have out your chat. This was what the Oak licensed, what made it so special. It was where you could converse at ease, women as well as men.

And here another aspect of the Oak's atmosphere needs to be noted. For all the names, or should that be classification, of the two bars – Public and Saloon/Lounge – people moved with ease between them. Yes, you tended to sit in the Lounge if you wanted a quiet chat, whereas the Public was more habituated to loud banter. And Edie's lunchtime meals were served only in the Lounge. But for all that, the Oak wasn't a place that endorsed distinctions. To say that the English pub tends to replicate the class system is hardly novel. Public, Lounge, Ladies (intended as a refuge for women who would otherwise never enter a pub), Jug & Bottle, usually a passageway for those who preferred to call in with a jug, typically enamel, have it filled with beer and carried home for the 'maister's' dinner, often by a child. You hardly ever see this nowadays, though when I was younger the Jug & Bottle was still in regular demand. And many of the larger pubs had non-smoking lounges. The architecture of pubs, including interior furnishings, has often enough been surveyed, frequently very well. Orwell's lovely essay, 'The Moon in the Water', tells you much about pub atmosphere in this regard.

But for Orwell, as for so many, pubs were essentially male preserves. What made the Oak so remarkable, wasn't merely that women were familiar presences in the Saloon/Lounge but they were at ease in the Public Bar, too, or even standing in the passage.

My guess is that pre-war middle-class women would rarely if ever have visited pubs, unless, that is, they were with husband or partner. And even then they would have felt out of place, or plain embarrassed at the very thought of being seen going into or exiting a drinking den, as I suppose they thought of a pub as being. During the war itself there was a certain degree of loosening up, especially among working women or ones who were with visiting GIs, or who, in that peculiar phrase, 'were no better than they should be', and this expanded in the post-war years. My mother, though, never felt at ease in a pub until her late years, and in earlier life, if she did go into one, it was only when persuaded to do so by my father, and she always looked self-conscious, out-of-place, while there.

The first time I saw a woman on her own in any pub was in nineteen fifty-four when, greatly daring (I was seventeen) I accompanied a slightly older friend into Soho's 'French Pub', as Dean Street's York Minster was and is still called, and while he went to the bar I gazed in wonderment around the smallish room at men and women in various stages of drunkenness, behaving in a manner that both shocked and thrilled my suburban soul.

Nothing that I ever saw in The Royal Oak could compare with that evening. And yet the pub in Villa Street definitely exuded an air of louche, tolerant inclusiveness. Hence, Hedgehog Bill. 'Allow twenty years for the Provinces' architectural historians are supposed to say, meaning that styles always take a number of years to spread from London. If sexual intercourse began in nineteen sixty-three, then so, *mutatis mutandis,* did the widespread use of pubs by women; and by the time Derek and Edie became tenants of the Oak, the pub was welcoming in a wide variety of women. Perhaps the presence of Edie behind the bar had something to do with this. No, cancel 'perhaps'. Edie was a terrific presence. Not, I need to add, in any way the kind of dragon who features in a good deal of popular art of the period. Nor did she in any way resemble Dickens's Mrs Lupin. She was on the short side, always neatly dressed – she especially favoured dark blue sweaters and grey skirts – with a squarish, attractive face, eyes that crinkled with laughter, and a wide smile, though if she disapproved of something done or said, her look would shift into a steady stare of serious dislike. Women as well as men felt safe in her presence. You wanted to please her. Of all the regulars only Bob begrudged her regular appearance behind the bar, and this was because she had no time for his churlishness.

She was very unlike the only other landlady I'd known at all well. Eileen – I never knew her surname – with her husband, Norman, ran The Queen's Head (aka 'The Nob') at Reading in the early nineteen-sixties. The couple had previously been part of the restaurant and drinks team at 'Royal' Ascot (Eileen was insistent on the prefix), and while Norman was affable and easy-going, largely I suspect because of the number of brandies he put away, Eileen was frostily grand. Her bosom helped. It was enormous, that bosom, and as Eileen favoured a succession of dresses with scooped-out tops, it was always on show. It was buttressed and braced, wide and deep enough you felt to support a fully-laid table for two, and regularly gave off clouds of rose-petal scented talcum powder which Eileen was rumoured to apply at half-hourly intervals from a canister kept beneath the counter in the Lounge Bar.

The Lounge was where Eileen held court, favouring her clients with stories of various bits of royalty and their doings at Ascot, of the truly thrilling conversational passages of arms between Lord So-and-So and the Earl of wherever it was, or of the strange habits of certain, not-to-be-named members of the Tory Cabinet. And while she unrolled each fascinating anecdote, she held aloft, between the first two fingers of her right hand, nails painted blood-red, a lengthy black cigarette holder containing a gold-tipped 'cocktail' cigarette, all the while sipping Babycham – topped up with a discreet splash of gin – from a wide-rimmed glass.

Meanwhile in the Public Bar, Norman entertained various cronies of the turf, all of them laughing louder as the drinks – mostly brandy and soda – went down, though he paused whenever asked to pull a pint for one of the world of the outer dark. I had nothing against Norman. He was always friendly, the beer (Symonds) was reasonably good, and he, or someone, kept the pub clean. I heard that not long after Pauline and I left Reading the poor man had to be taken away, (DTs). Of Eileen's later life, history does not report.

One thing is for sure. She would not have approved of the Oak's Ladies Darts Team. Eileen would have thought it frightfully *infra dig*. During Chris and Margaret's stewardship the Oak had no such team. Darts was played in the Public Bar, by women as well as by men, but there weren't any team competitions. In earlier days, I heard from Chris, the skittle alley had been much used. The Oak had its own team, and was, I think, in a league made up of at least a dozen pub sides in the area. But by the late 'sixties, skittles, for whatever reason, was no longer popular. Pub games moved indoors. Inter-pub rivalries had lessened, and now cribbage, gin rummy, whist, dominoes, shove-ha'penny, table quoits, and very occasional games of backgammon were set up. As for chess, that was only played in the Oak when Ian's brother, Don, was home from the sea, and games were confined to the Saloon.

Card games mostly featured at weekends. Saturday night was the big one. Couples would settle at a favourite table early in the evening and commence play, often enough not finishing until the bell rang for closing time.

'Time Gentlemen Please' had ceased to be the cry that brought evenings to their end, though as a special favour to me Chris did once call out the words. This was when an Indian friend from America was staying at our house. Flight Lt. B.N. Burjorjee, DFC (ret'd), 'Bandi' as he was familiarly known, rejoiced in all things British. From Washington DC he sent to London for his clothes. Austin Reed supplied his shirts and raincoat, as they did his suits and jackets, he smoked Senior Service, and he would not drink bourbon. Moreover, he drove a Morris Minor. He would be staying with us for a week, of course wanted to sample English beer, and expressed the wish to be in a pub at closing time in order to hear Mine Host cry the words that would bring the evening to its end.

The evening before I was due to take Bandi round to the Oak I dropped in to ask Chris if he'd be prepared to do the necessary. Chris agreed. And at ten-thirty the following evening, and to the wonderment of the regulars, Chris bellowed **TIME GENTLEMEN PLEASE.**

94

Bandi was entranced. 'You see,' he said to me, as we walked home, 'it is as I say to the chaps in Washington. England is the country of unchanging tradition.'

Saturday nights at the Oak were generally agreed to be when you were expected to look your best. Ladies had their hair permed, wore two-piece costumes or, less often, formal dresses (some even had a nosegay, bought for them by their husbands); their male partners, who had all week gone from home to work in boiler-suits or overalls, now appeared in 'Sunday best' suits, with collar and tie, some with waistcoats, and quite often cuff-links, shoes highly polished; and as they sat down they produced unopened packets of cigarettes which they placed at their elbows, silver lighters atop. A moment or two to settle, to exchange formal compliments, then one or other of the men would rise and go for drinks – pints for the males and, for their ladies, glasses of gin and tonic (or bitter lemon): toasts would be proposed, glasses clinked, and the evening proper could commence.

Come mid-evening Edie would circulate with platters of sliced pork pie, cubes of cheddar cheese topped by silver onions and slices of gherkin secure on cocktail sticks, and, occasionally, thick rings of cold black pudding. And perhaps the man from Grimsby, in boater, white jacket and wicker basket, would arrive with varieties of shellfish. And although Derek seldom changed from his yellow pullover, on Saturdays he at least added a dark green scarf, tied loosely at the neck, to his outfit.

Ah, those Saturday nights! In the late 'fifties, when I went as often as possible to Eel Pie Island, an eyot in the Thames at Twickenham where Sandy Brown's superb jazz band were semi-resident, they usually included at some stage in the evening a High Life number which Brown himself had composed and which he sang in his unique, gravelly, jazzman's voice, 'Ev'rybody Loves Saturday Night.' And at Beeston's Royal Oak, too, everybody loved Saturday night.

7: Darts and Dodgers

Games of darts weren't forbidden on Saturday nights, but neither were they encouraged. And after eight o'clock tables were positioned in front of the board so that playing the game was impossible. Saturday nights were for table games or for people grouped together in conversation. The juke box was turned down and although a certain amount of beery singing was tolerated in the passage, in both Public and Lounge bars the loudest sounds you heard were of people laughing at each other's anecdotes.

On other nights, however, the darts board was in regular use. Anyone could play. Derek kept a set of darts behind the bar though most people brought their own. The majority of the players were men – except for Wednesdays. Wednesday was Ladies' Night. That was when men had to watch, and applaud. There was much to applaud. 'Darts, Grace!' 'Good arrers, Doreen!' The Ladies' Darts team were the pride of the Oak. For several years running they were champions of the local league. I can't remember how many matches were played in the course of the season, but I do know that away matches were especially looked forward to. The team would be accompanied by a swelling number of supporters, husbands, boy-friends, others, some of whom went by car to Kegworth or West Leake or Rempstone … wherever … flags and knitted scarves hanging from the windows or wrapped round the car's aerial; but the majority favoured travelling by coach. On these occasions a thirty-two seater was supplied by the local Barton's Bus Company, and early evening on alternate Wednesdays throughout autumn and winter it would be waiting outside the pub ready to take the always smartly dressed team and their spruced-up fans to their opponents' pub.

The return journey was always planned so as to get the coach back to the Oak for one last drink before closing time. And as the Ladies had invariably triumphed the mood would be festive. Horns honked as a cavalcade of wheeled transport rolled up Villa Street. 'Get your rattles ready,' Arthur Crouch would say, or, on the rare occasions when the team had been defeated and players and supporters filed moodily in, 'Never mind, it's only a game. A pint of Shippos will set you right.' And he'd fire off a gruff laugh.

Fortunately, Arthur's laugh, and his words of consolation, were not often required. When for the third consecutive year the Ladies won the league, by a country mile, so it was said, and the small silver cup retained its pride of place on the bar counter, Beeston's mayor consented to make a public presentation, an event which a local newspaper agreed to cover. Someone, I think it may have been Harold, suggested, probably tongue-in-cheek, that bunting ought to be hung along Villa Street, but this was vetoed partly because nobody could come up with a possible supplier but more because there seemed to be general agreement that this particular mayor, a supplier of electrical goods, was a grumpy sod who only held the post because his turn had come up. Buggins.

Still, it was an enjoyable evening. The mayor arrived by official car, and the chauffeur, Tony Radd, one of the Oak's regulars, was given a loud cheer as he stepped from behind the driver's seat and opened the rear door for the mayor, whose emergence into the light of evening was met with near silence. Tony then held the pub's street door open for his mayorship, as someone called him, we followed him down the passage, and Derek, in his yellow sweater, indicated from his place behind the bar that the company should turn left. There, in the Public Bar, placed strategically around the darts board, stood the victorious Ladies; Doreen Spooner, by day part-owner of a shoe-shop and of an evening the Team's captain, holding the cup; and around them were gathered a sizeable number of their loyal supporters, beer glasses in hand.

The mayor read out a prepared speech about the achievement of the team helping to put Beeston on the map (how?), made some laboured and largely incomprehensible joke about how these lovely ladies had exchanged Cupid's arrow for piercing the heart of the darts board (nobody laughed), added that their triumph went to show how talent could be found in unlikely places (somebody muttered 'what do you mean, unlikely, you berk?'), and concluded by saying that in future years the team might prove an example to us all. (How?).

From the passage, a voice, stirred to ironic eloquence, called out, 'Where did you find *him,* Tony?' a remark Derek tried to cover up by asking us to raise our glasses and toast the Ladies Team; so we did. And after that the mayor departed and the evening went on its way.

Next evening I was shown a short piece in the local rag's front page. Under the headline, *Didn't They Do Well?* was a murky photograph of some of the Ladies grouped round the darts board, and beneath that a few lines of newsprint about the team, which managed to misspell most of their names as well as those of 'mine hosts', who were identified as 'Derrick and Deirdre' and thanked for lifting the spirits of the town. (Ho! Ho!). Of the mayor's speech there was no mention, though his presence was noted.

***

I don't know who the passage barracker of the mayoral oration was but it may well have been 'Speedy' – the only name I had for one of the passage regulars who was in most nights. Most nights when he was at large, anyway. According to Harold, Speedy was a window-cleaner equally celebrated for the rapidity with which he cleaned – or didn't clean – windows, and the speed with which he made off with items he was able to retrieve from windows left ajar or ones that were insecurely closed.

He was less speedy at avoiding the long arm of the law. As a result, having progressed from cautions to fines to community service he now spent periods in Oakham Open Prison. Speedy was incorrigible but relatively harmless. Most of what he nicked was soon recovered, the cops after all knew who they were after; and quite a few of us wondered whether stealing wasn't for him a kind of game. He always claimed, though, that football was his favourite sport. 'I'll tell you one thing, John,' he once said to me.

'Bit of advice, this is. If you're in Oakham, ask to play in goal. There's some smashing views all around.'

For all I know, Speedy may have thought that all male regulars of the Oak spent some time in prison. It was where you went to carry on the conversation. A bit like the Oak itself, though without beer. He bore his captors no ill will. 'Only doing their job,' he said.

Simple Simon was another cheerful miscreant. Like Speedy, Simon always did his best to look smartly dressed – fresh-pressed trousers, clean shirt and tie – but unlike the errant window-cleaner, Simon preferred to use the Lounge rather than the passage. He was a Friday night regular, always wearing a too-long check sports jacket, the same chocolate-brown gabardines, and he always had a smile as wide and genial as George Formby's, to whom he bore a strong facial resemblance. Moreover he had similar slicked-back hair. But instead of a ukulele, Simon toted a suitcase. He'd arrive sometime in the earlier part of the evening, buy himself a pint, then set it down on a table in the Lounge, careful to leave enough space for him to hoist the suitcase into position.

'What's fell off the back of a lorry this week, Simon?' Arthur Crouch might ask.

'I got some smashing goods here, believe me.' And Simon, having taken a lengthy pull at his beer, would undo the strap that held the suitcase together, and throw the lid up. 'Socks like you did never see. Vests, gentleman's underpants. Go anywhere in them I tell you.' Simon's accent, as well as his vocabulary, was a strange blend of English and some foreign language – possibly Polish. (There were rumours that he'd escaped from that country soon after the end of the war.) 'Honest, Gents, these what I have tonight is the goods.' Fenced goods, of course. Most evenings Simon made a few sales, after which he'd close the suitcase and head for the next pub.

On several Friday nights, though, as he made to leave the Lounge, his exit would be blocked by a uniformed policeman.

'What you got in that suitcase, Simon?'

'Just off on my holidays, officer.'

'You never spoke a truer word.'

And off to Beeston Police Station Simon would go, wishing us all pleasant dreams before he left.

***

'There was no harm in Simon,' most of the regulars agreed, though George Healey 'couldn't be doing with his like.' George was a plumber whose severest criticism was reserved for anyone whom he claimed had 'no work in him.' Among those he condemned for this failing were, of course, both Simon and Speedy, and also Sid Gams. Sid was an under-groundsman at the University, responsible for a variety of menial tasks – marking out pitches, putting up goal nets, mowing and the like. He was forbidden from attending to the cricket squares. These were cared for by the head groundsman, Sid Sprey, and as he and his underling shared their Christian names, I provided Sid Gams with the soubriquet of Sub Sid. It stuck, though I felt a twinge of guilt about this, given that Sub Sid was, as Australians say, a few bricks short of a load. But he himself was delighted by it. I think he felt it conferred an identity on him beyond that of University Parks and Gardens employee.

Sub Sid always stood in the passage at the Oak, frequently arriving by tractor early of a weekday evening in his overalls, prepared to tell anyone who would listen, as well as those who didn't, of his day's labours. 'A bloody caper I've had of it,' he'd begin, and run through tales of line-whitening that had gone wrong (meaning that he'd failed to keep to anything like a straight line) goalposts that had proved buggers to put up (meaning that he'd hung the cross bar the wrong way round so that the net hooks were pitch-side) and on one memorable occasion the misbehaviour of the tractor's steering system (meaning that he'd backed the machine onto the running-track where it stalled just as a competition race was due to start.)

Soon after that mishap we discovered that Sub Sid wasn't qualified to drive the tractor off-campus. One evening he came barrelling up Villa Street, five minutes late for his first pint of the day, bashed into a van pulling out from the snooker hall lower down the street, and although technically it was the other driver's responsibility, police questioning unearthed the information that Sub Sid didn't have a proper driving licence. Fortunately, Sid Sprey spoke up for him, as did several of the *Oak's* regulars, and he was let off with a caution. But his tractor driving days were at an end and from then on the poor man was on digging, seeding, hoeing, and such like duties. You'd see him humping heavy sacks about the University grounds, and as he had some form of curvature of the spine, he cut a sad figure as he went on his way, looking every inch a Millet peasant as re-imagined by Josef Herman.

Quite a few of us clubbed together to buy him a second-hand bicycle so he could still get to the Oak of an evening, but there were several abstentions when the hat was passed around. Among them George Healey was foremost. George was a burly figure, habitué of the Public Bar and once or twice a recruit to the football team for which I played, The Sunday Academicals. We were a hopeless lot, most of the team claiming to use the matches as a way of getting rid of Saturday night hangovers, but with George at centre-half we gained a certain notoriety. Rumour had it that at some time in the past he had played for Notts County reserves, and hearing of this we asked if his playing days were over. If not, then we'd be flattered if George would agree to turn out for us whenever the need arose. We – that is those of us who drank in the Oak – took to buying him a pint or two, and after several weeks of this he said alright.

George's acceptance came just in time for him to be drafted into the team for the coming Sunday, when we would be facing a team about which we knew nothing but greatly feared. The Percy Arms, a pub in Finsbury Park, London, sported a football side which operated under the *soi-disant* management of my friend, the poet and novelist, Barry Cole, he whose charms had been lost on Chris and Margaret's daughter. Now, some five or six years later, he and I had arranged for this side, which included, so Barry airily informed me, a trainer and a sub (or twelfth man), to make the journey from north London to Beeston, where I had booked them into a hall of residence for Saturday night. The Londoners arrived by coach early evening, we took them to the Oak, plied them with drink, and by closing time they were, most of them, in various stages of advanced inebriation.

The following morning some of us called for them and guided them down to the side of the Trent where the match was to be played. It was a cold, raw, windy morning, and although our left-winger, a teetotaller in the history department, announced that he was feeling 'pretty perky,' I doubt that many of us were enthusiastic about our prospects, especially when the opposition emerged from their changing room in a proper, all-blue strip. (Chelsea cast-offs we later learnt.) Even the sub was in blue, and the trainer came complete with bucket and sponge. As for Barry, he wore a sheepskin coat, had donned a large fedora, and was smoking a cigar. Eat your heart out, Malcolm Allison.

He gathered his team about him for a brief pep talk, which was probably along the lines of those regularly delivered by the famous Forest manager, Johnny Carey to his excellent eleven of the 1960s. 'Just spray it about a bit, lads.' The words worked well enough for Forest, at that time one of the most entertaining teams in the old First Division. I used to go to most of their home games, standing in the enclosure, and even now I can recall many of that side. Peter Grummit in goal ('brave and innocent' according to the *Observer*) 'Tank' Hindley and John Winfield at full-back; half-backs, Whitehead, McLintock, the team's captain, and the splendidly lithe Henry Newton, and, among the forwards, Wignall, an old-fashioned centre-forward of the kind called 'rugged', John Barnwell (previously of Arsenal) and, on the wing, Ian Storey Moore, one of the finest of attacking wingers, fleet-footed, full of guile, but kicked out of the game by various licensed thugs with nicknames such as Butcher and Chopper.

Meanwhile, as Barry delivered his instructions, the opposition – us – stood about shivering in our crumpled, grass-stained white shirts and black shorts (most of them), though a good friend in the English department made do with a pair of below the knee cut-offs he'd bought, second-hand, from the local Army and Navy store, which gave the impression that he was auditioning for the role of Sanders of the River, though without pith helmet and butterfly net, while our goalkeeper, an American research student who rejoiced under the name of Floyd J. Weintraub Jnr., was clad in a black padded windcheater, long grey woolly pants, and an American footballer's leather headgear supplemented by ear muffs. Only our guest player, George, in a black-and-white striped football shirt, black shorts, and a pair of high-sided boots with reinforced toecaps, looked as though he was prepared for serious business. And so it turned out.

The referee – supplied by one of the local amateur leagues – blew his whistle, The Percy Arms centre-forward made what I believe is called a darting run at George, and for the first but by no means last time the trainer had to be called onto the pitch. George hadn't moved, he simply let the centre-forward bounce off him. After prolonged application of the sponge, the centre-forward was helped to his feet and led tottering away.

And so it went on. By half-time the visitors' sub had come on and gone off, as had two others. The final score was 6–2 in our favour and the only reason The Percy Arms scored at all was entirely due to us. Their first goal occurred when, with a confident cry of 'Yours', Sanders of the River, who was extremely short-sighted, sent a back pass to Floyd J Weintraub Jnr., not being able to see that the goalkeeper had chosen that very moment to go behind his goal in order to smoke some waccy baccy provided for him by his girlfriend. Opinion was divided as to who had been more at fault in allowing The Percy Arms open their account.

The second goal led to even sharper disagreements between Sanders and Floyd J. Weintraub Jnr., each blaming the other. The facts are these. Not long before the match came to an end, Floyd J Weintraub Jnr., still smarting from what he regarded as the unfair charge of having abandoned his goal without leave, was called upon to take a goal kick. He prepared for this with some care, running at the ball from at least ten yards before delivering it a tremendous blow. The mud-slathered ball shot off his foot at an oblique angle, and with the squelching sound a rotten melon might make when hurled against brick, thudded into the head of Sanders of the River, who was at that moment straightening up from a discreet fit of vomiting. Sanders now fell silently to earth, he knew not where, the ball ricocheted toward goal and Floyd J. Weintraub

Jnr., who had been hoping to resume his search for a reefer he had earlier discarded in long grass, collapsed in hysterical laughter. Meanwhile, the 'leather spheroid,' as commentators of yore preferred to call a football, entered our net.

Afterwards, as we gathered, most of us, in the Oak, we thanked George for his massive contribution to our unexpected victory. What had he thought of the opposition?

'There's no work in them,' George said. 'Anyway, I hate bloody Chelsea.'

He also hated Ron Goodwin. Well, hated may be pitching it too high, but then George was convinced that Ron pitched it too high. Ron was a senior university groundsman who was allowed to live in a small gatehouse at the edge of campus. On duty he wore a dark, official-looking jacket, and he often wore it off-duty, too, in cold weather adding a duffle-coat. A badge of office sporting the University crest was pinned to the trilby he wore on evenings out. He was, I suppose, a jobsworth, though he rarely bothered me and I couldn't see why he so irritated George, who wasn't after all employed by the University. But George reckoned that even in the pub Ron liked to tell drinkers when he thought they'd had enough and that they should be thinking of going to their homes.

Not surprisingly, Ron also got up Sub Sid's nose. George told me of a passage of arms between the pair of them. One evening Ron informed Sub Sid that he'd had quite enough to drink, and should be on his bike. 'I hates you, Goodwin,' Sid had replied and taken a swing at his oppressor. Ron, so George told me, had some boxing skills, picked up during his days of service in the navy. He blocked Sub Sid's clumsy attempt at a blow, caught the other man's wrist, and said, 'I'll break your arm, you little worm.'

'Leave him be,' George said. 'You're bigger than him.' Which was true.

Ron had apparently realised that taking George on wouldn't be a good idea, said something about not wanting to dirty his hands, and pushed his way out of the pub.

'I ought to have gone after him,' George said, 'but I'd left it too long to lay one on the pompous git.'

But what he seemed most bothered by was that as a result of his intercession Sub Sid took to regarding him as a friend, a form of flattery George could do without.

Sub Sid also thought of me as a friend. After all, I'd given him his name. He once stopped me in the street and held up a large plastic bag for my inspection. 'Guppies,' he said. 'Three on 'em. I'll be along to the Oak once I've got 'em in the tank.'

Keeping freshwater fish, I learnt later that evening, was Sub Sid's passion. He even made aquariums for them, which he sold to other enthusiasts. The news delighted me. I wanted an aquarium for Ben, hoping to interest my young son in pond and river life, and I asked Sub Sid if he could construct one for me. Yes, he could, and I could pay him when I went to his house to collect it. How big? Two feet by one by one, I suggested. Done.

Two weeks later I went round to his council house and gladly paid him for the small, well-constructed fish tank, as he called it, though I intended it for newts and water weed. Sub Sid showed me his other tanks, all of them his own work. There were eight of them, variously sized, placed all around the room, on tables and shelves, most of them containing fish: guppies, sticklebacks, and, in the largest, a pair of dace. Some had been bought from a local shop specialising in river fish, but most came from the Trent, or the Beeston Cut, or Attenborough Nature Reserve and its attendant gravel pits. Sid, it turned out, was a keen angler. As he bent in front of his tanks I saw how his face lit up, the absorbed pleasure with which he explained what weights you needed for what fish, what hooks, which bait, and how you should care for them. And hearing his throat tighten with excitement as he talked on, I felt ashamed of my previous amused condescension toward him.

8: Change in the Air

Change was coming to Beeston, and it was increasingly visible, even obtrusive.

Early in the nineteen-seventies the town council announced plans for an inner ring road. Nottingham had one so why not Beeston? It was pointed out by concerned citizens that not only was Nottingham a large city but that in the inner city the major new road slicing through some streets of Georgian houses had already been pronounced the ugliest street in Europe. To propose a ring road for Beeston was quite simply a case of *folie de grandeur*. Not to put too fine a point on it, it was absurd. In response to these hostile observations the council argued – well, asserted – that there was nothing wrong with ambition. But an inner ring road would have the effect of burying much of Beeston under concrete, we said. You might as well announce plans to turn the High Street into Pall Mall.

We started a petition against the council's proposal. Just about everyone in the Oak signed although Bob refused. 'You can't stop progress,' he said. After a few weeks we had over two thousand signatures. The council announced a public meeting, to be held at the Town Hall. As the public chamber only had room for about fifty people, we proposed moving to a larger space. This proposal was refused but an annexe was wired up so that the debate could be heard by all those who attended. Some two hundred of us did. The petition was presented and the debate to discuss the merits of the ring road then began.

Councillor Clifford (Cons.) opened the proceedings by stating that the trouble with petitions was that they only put one side of the argument. Much laughter ensued which caused Councillor Woodward (Cons.) to announce that in his opinion the public was just like any other mob. At this point laughter turned to hysteria. Councillor Woodward then proposed clearing the public from the room. It was pointed out that you could hardly have a public debate without the public being present. Councillor Woodward dropped into his seat and refused to speak again that evening. At the end of the debate, the Council proposed putting the plans out to independent assessment. Proposal accepted. A few weeks later the plans were withdrawn, though not in time to save Middle Street, a road of some charm, from destruction.

Bob was right. You couldn't stop progress. We'd saved Beeston from an inner ring road but the town was becoming a different place. Shops along the High Street changed hands and changed identity. A dress shop, a shoe shop, a gentleman's retailer, all became electronics stores. Curry's, Rumbelow's, Dixon's. Fridges, freezers, hi-fi stacks now stood in windows that had once displayed suits and frocks and underwear. (Only *Sheila's Hats* retained both name and its display of headwear that looked as though they had been created some time in the Edwardian era. Nobody was ever seen entering or exiting the shop, and rumours abounded as to its owner. Perhaps she had been dead these many years. Perhaps the shop was a front for an illegal gambling den.

But the major changes were of a different kind. When Pauline and I had arrived in Beeston toward the end of the nineteen-sixties the town boasted a parish church, a rather handsome Methodist church, and no fewer than twenty-two chapels. I know, I walked right round Beeston, counting them. Ebenezer, Seventh-Day Adventist, Congregational, Primitive Methodist, Baptist .... By then many of them had shut their doors for the last time and as the decade turned so I began to notice pews and other impedimenta standing on the pavement outside junk shops, Boden's in particular. Soon, the buildings themselves were up for sale and before long became car showrooms, carpet warehouses, a timber store, or were converted into various kinds of living quarters. Astonishing, how quickly the change occurred. By the end of the decade only the Anglican church and three Methodist chapels remained. Beeston's past was being erased.

Then the factories began to close. Myford's Mill, Ariel Pressings, Attenborough's Mill, and, most grievous of all as far as the Oak was concerned, the lace factory on Villa Street. At least two of these buildings went up in flames. Pauline and I stood at the top of our road, watched those fires against the night sky, and thought of Turner and Wright of Derby.

Opinion in the Oak was that all the fires had been started deliberately. 'After last drinks,' someone suggested. And it was agreed that the blaze which reduced the lace factory opposite the pub to a jumble of charred beams and blackened brick must have been an inside job. The mill had closed a month or so earlier and by the time of the fire all the machinery had been sold off. What burned was an empty shell. 'Insurance money,' was the whisper. 'Ask no questions ....'

A miracle that the Oak had escaped without damage, was the general opinion, but Arthur Crouch, our authority on such matters, thought otherwise. 'They'll have made sure to smash the glass before they started. Best way to avoid an explosion. The lads who attended towd me the fire started the far side of the factory, making bleddy sure the pub got off wi'out trouble. A wise dog don't piss in its own basket.'

'Well, lucky for the Oak.'

'And lucky for the street. Whoever was behind the fire made sure to spare the 'ouses alongside. That's where people live. Do 'arm to them and the Law'd be down on 'em in a big way.'

In the event there was a low-level enquiry, on which the *Post* reported. An old building, security relaxed now the factory was closed, accidents happen. The insurance was paid. Case closed.

Nevertheless the fires affected Derek and Edie's trade. Lace workers no longer came in at the end of their afternoon shift and others from the closed-down factories nearby also became absent friends. Then the council moved its clerical offices and as a result Edie had fewer requests for lunchtime meals.

One evening Harold and I met as we walked to the pub, each, we told the other, dropping in for a quick one. 'Heard the rumour,' Harold said, and when I looked enquiringly at him, 'Derek and Edie are leaving us.'

I had, in fact, already heard it from Bill Cole, though I'd not taken much notice. Bill lived on Queen's Road, Beeston's lower through road, and his house was more or less opposite a large pub called The Queen's Head, another Shipstone's House. I'd never been into it though Bill had told me several tales of its activities, mostly to do with evenings when he played there with a jazz trio of bass, keyboard, and guitar. On one occasion a jazz follower, known on the circuit as Dapper Dan on account of his impeccable suits and snap-brim trilby, had at the end of the evening produced a revolver and, standing on the pub's raised steps, fired off some blanks. The result was far from what Dapper Dan had intended. All the alarms in nearby shops began shrilling, the police were almost immediately on the scene, and Dapper Dan had to be hidden under a table while the boys in blue sniffed around.

From all Bill told me I decided that the Queen's didn't sound like Derek and Edie's kind of place. But I'd reckoned without Beeston Boilers. This was a factory employing a large number of both skilled and semi-skilled workers no further than fifty yards down a side road from where the pub stood, and many of the factory's employees lived on or directly off the Queen's Road. And there were in addition a number of smaller businesses nearby, which in total amounted to considerably more than the Oak's potential clientele. It made sense.

Sure enough, at the end of the week, Derek announced that he and his family would be leaving in a month's time. 'You'll be in good hands,' he said, 'I've met the new couple, John and Dawn, shown them around, they know the business, moving from another Shippo's in Long Eaton. I warned them about you lot but they're not bothered.'

Then, with a smile and a wink, 'He used to be in the navy, so watch your step, all of you, or you'll be swinging from the yard arm.'

'He'll need a steel hawser for Bob,' someone said.

'Bob can go overboard,' Derek said, 'do as shark food.'

There was some laughter, but it was subdued.

As we walked away from the pub, Ted, who was with me said, 'End of an era, that is.'

I wanted to be loyal to Chris and Margaret. 'We've been lucky,' I said, 'they followed a good pair.'

'Third time unlucky,' Ted said.

In the weeks before Derek and Edie left I made a point of calling at what was to be their new pub. I was curious to see what they'd be going to. The Queen's was a good deal more spacious than the Oak. The Lounge in particular looked well-kept, its dark oak tables and padded wooden chairs polished and unscuffed, almost, I thought, forbidding. As for the Public Bar, it held not only a juke box but two fruit machines, though it seemed to me even chillier than the Lounge, frosted glass windows somehow reminiscent of a funeral parlour. I hoped Derek and Edie would be happy here, but I had my doubts. Or was it that I simply didn't want them gone from the Oak? Probably. No, it was the truth. I didn't at all like the thought of the pub on Villa Street without the pair of them. Loyal though I was to the memory of Chris and Margaret, I accepted that Derek and Edie had brought new energy to the pub, richer supplies of laughter; they'd been at once tolerant of the off-beat characters the pub now welcomed, but at the same time had, however unobtrusively, been in control. Under them the pub flourished, not merely because it was so often full but because it became a place where all sorts of people could feel at ease, could feel they truly belonged. They could sit to talk, to play games, to debate issues from little to vast, with the result that a genuine, surprisingly wide-ranged community established itself. And the Oak exemplified order in variety. I couldn't imagine anyone wanting, let alone daring, to take issue with Derek and Edie, let alone challenge what they'd accomplished, what they'd made of the Oak. They were naturals.

The Saturday prior to their going, the pub was open all day, though Derek announced he'd be closing early. He wanted time to welcome John and Dawn into their new premises, help them settle in, and have the pub ready for them to open the street door at the due hour on next Monday morning. And in the meantime he and Edie would be putting all their goods and chattels in storage while they went down to Hampshire for a week, visiting family, looking up old haunts, and preparing themselves for life after the Oak.

Of course we'd tipped in money for a farewell gift. Two, in fact. Binoculars for Derek – 'Help you see across to the far side of the Queen's Public Bar' – and, for Edie, a black-bead necklace. 'I hope that didn't come from Speedy,' Derek said, and Speedy, who was free to join in the celebrations said, 'No chance of that mate, it's out of my class.'

We toasted them, someone called out 'Speech,' and Harold, I think it was, said, 'Send for the Mayor of Beeston.'

When the fake boos and jeers died away, Derek told us that he and his wife had enjoyed their years at the Oak, were pleased to have met us all, and looked forward to seeing us at the Queen's if we fancied going off-course for a drink. Edie accepted help in handing round the accustomed salvers of sandwiches and slices of pork pie, and we settled to more drink before Derek, for once, shouted 'Time Gentlemen Please.' Adding 'Ten minutes for drinking up then off you go.' An old pals moment, that, one when we could all join in a feeling of comradeship.

I raised my glass to Derek, took in his familiar yellow pullover with the special effects green cravat, and as I met his eyes I realised he was looking back steadily at me, and I had a sudden moment of insight. This evening meant much more to us than to him. There was nothing cold or calculating in Derek's stare, but nor, I knew then, was he feeling any great sense of a parting, of loss. He had been an exemplary tenant, but that was what he'd set himself to be. And now he'd had enough of the Oak. Time to move on, to make a success of running another pub. That he'd do it I had no doubt. And when he came to the end of his years being landlord of the Queen's he'd leave that pub with as little regret as he was now leaving the Oak. You couldn't stop change, and why should you try? Change was the only constant.

Part Three: John and Dawn

1: All Shipshape

'Y ou'll be alright here,' Harold said.

He held his half-drunk glass of mixed up to the uncertain light of the passageway. 'Keeps a decent pint, and the place is spotless.'

Actually, I found the smell of cleaning fluid that seemed to come from every corner of the pub a bit too much, and said so.

'Used to swabbing down decks, that's why,' Harold said. 'Get yourself a pint and come and join me.' And unusually for him he went through to the Lounge.

At that moment the pub's new landlord emerged from the Public Bar, bucket of water in hand. 'I've been giving the windows a going over,' he said, as I introduced myself and, having given his right hand a vigorous rub on his overalls, he took mine. 'The grime of ages on them, if you ask me.'

As I knew that Derek and Edie regularly cleaned all windows in the pub, I didn't warm to this implied criticism of the Oak's former tenants. But I was to find in the coming weeks that John verged on the obsessive about cleanliness. As Harold once remarked, God would have a hard time keeping up with him. Put your pint down on the bar counter and he'd immediately reach for a rag in order to wipe away any excess moisture. A sign above the bar read, **Please, NO smoking in this area,** and he was forever going from room to room, taking up ashtrays, shaking the contents into a small pail, scrubbing them clean with a damp cloth, and then banging them back down in the dead centre of the table.

It ought to have been off-putting, and for some, Bob especially, it was. But against this, John was a man of affable, open manner, who soon came to know each drinker's preference, and who enjoyed conversation. He was a shade under middle height and according to Harold, whom I now joined in the Lounge – 'Best keep out of our new man's way when he's busy with the mop' – had for several years been a welterweight champion in the navy.

How Harold knew this, I'm not sure, because John rarely talked about himself and he kept no trophies on show. But it was true. I discovered this soon enough, because a drummer I regularly played with, Don Ripley, who had at one time been in the army, where he had won several prizes for his performances in the ring, looked John's name up for me – records were kept of inter-service competitions – and confirmed that John had indeed been not merely regional but national champion for two years running. 'Don't get into a barney with him,' Don said, 'not if you want to keep your teeth. And without them your days as a trumpet-man are over.'

I have to say that at first glance you'd not think of John as a fighter. No cauliflower ear, no bent nose, no sign of split lips. But I suppose he'd worn a head-shield. From time to time I wondered whether to bring up the subject of boxing but I never did. Always willing to join in banter, John was nevertheless loath to talk about his days in the ring. Nor did he drink. Bendigo, I once called him, but he looked at me quizzically, perhaps uncomprehendingly, and I decided not to enlighten him.

He invariably wore a white roll-neck sweater, perhaps in homage to his navy days, though it had the unintended effect of reminding me of a moment from the filmed version of *The Cruel Sea,* one of the many films made in the nineteen-fifties which extolled the quiet heroism of the British at war. In one scene of this particular film, Jack Hawkins, as a ship's skipper, stands alone on the bridge of his destroyer where he broods with impeccably furrowed brow over men he has no choice but to plough over rather than rescue from their sunk craft (why, I can't recall); and as he broods in stoical dignity, he is joined by a junior officer, played by Bryan Forbes, who brings with him a mug and an expression of deep concern. 'Cocoa, sir?' he asks. Yes, really.

John's wife, Dawn, was a sweet-faced woman. Like her husband she was originally from Devon, and she plainly loved and admired him. In fact, they were a loving couple, who made a point of stroking each other's arms as they crossed behind the bar, and smiling as they met each other's gaze. Dawn said little but she was invariably ready to listen to customers as they reported their grievances to her – the state of the weather, the state of politics, the state of Nottingham's traffic. Dawn would nod sympathetically, tut when required, and, from her stool behind the bar, pull the complainant his pint of beer.

The stool was necessary because Dawn had a gammy leg, caused by a botched knee operation. As a result, she was forced to wear a steel caliper which obviously caused her acute discomfort. She could ease this by lessening the grip of the caliper, but to do this she had to raise a kind of latch on the caliper's side. Whenever she did this, either to give some rest to her leg or to improve speed of movement, there was a loud, and to be brutal, rather sickening click.

Inevitably, Dawn couldn't help in the pub as much as either Margaret or Edie had helped their husbands. She did her best to be of assistance, taking her turn in pulling pints and reaching for bottles beneath the counter, but there wasn't much else she could do round and about the pub. And cooking and serving lunchtime meals was, inevitably, beyond her. Given that the council offices had recently moved premises, this wasn't as great a setback as it would have been during those years when Edie's innovatory service brought in regular money. But as far as food was concerned, the Oak was now back to the days of crisps and pickled eggs. These latter were said to lurk in a large jar of mucky liquid which stood on one side of the bar, though I never heard of anyone daring to plumb its depths in search of hidden treasure.

Nor did the sellers of shellfish from Grimsby continue their weekend visits. The factories had closed and as they did so custom vanished. Saturday nights were losing their glamour. The Oak was still a good place to go for a drink and a chat, but the air of excitement that hung in the air, the eagerness with which people flung open the street door and stood for a moment, turning their heads from side to side, as though savouring the atmosphere, the buzz of conversation, the cannonades of laughter, all that had gone. John waited behind the bar, his look one of measured expectation, Dawn smiled – increasingly I thought there was something anxious about the smile – the pub was unfailingly clean and tidy, stools tucked under tables, ashtrays were kept spotless, the beer was unfailingly clean-tasting, and John had replaced the picture of the liquid-eyed beauty over the fireplace, which Edie had taken, with a three-masted schooner in full sail. All was, you could say, trim and shipshape, even allowing for the hulking presence of Bob, who like a beached snark still sat in his corner by the fireplace, bottles accumulating round his ankles as the evening wore on.

But it wasn't the same. It wasn't and it wouldn't be.

2: Not Worth It

'Where's Ian?' I asked John one evening, as he pulled my pint of mixed. 'I've not seen him for some while.' Then, realising he might not know who I meant, I said, 'He's usually in of an evening. He sits on the other side of the fireplace from Bob, but I've not seen him for a week or two.'

But John knew who Ian was. 'Our walking encyclopaedia,' he said. Then, 'Now you come to mention it, he's not been in of late. Ask in the Lounge.'

But nobody there could explain his absence, though someone suggested that he might be 'off on his holidays.'

'Don't be bleddy daft,' Arthur Crouch said, 'holiday from what? He ain't done a day's work in ten years or more.'

'A few more on us'll soon be on permanent holiday,' someone said, 'the way things are shaping up.'

There were nods and growls of agreement. Now that most of the local factories had closed, finding work in and around Beeston was increasingly difficult. Men went further afield in search of jobs, which of course meant that if successful they came home at later hours and were less likely to spend much time in the Oak. And as for their womenfolk, in the absence of secretarial or canteen work, they were more often than not filling their evenings with bar work or behind the counter of coffee bars that were beginning to appear along the High Street where McDonald's had recently opened a branch. Then Kentucky Fried Chicken arrived, and with those places to go to, the Oak lost most of the younger drinkers it had once attracted.

As for Ian, we soon enough discovered the reason for his prolonged absence. He'd been found lying in the street outside his house, and was now in hospital, not expected to come out alive. Years of heavy drinking and smoking had wrecked his health. Lung cancer? Cirrhosis of the liver? Heart?

A few weeks later came news of his death. A card of condolence was propped on the bar with an invitation to sign, and Harold volunteered to drop it in at his address.

'One down, ten to go,' Arthur said, but it was gallows humour. Even Bob seemed subdued.

***

At the end of the darts' season the Ladies' team disbanded. So many teams from other pubs had given up that the league, which at its height had consisted of sixteen teams, was by now down to seven. Some of the Oak's best players had handed in their darts because they now had evening work and didn't fancy being out every night of the week. And for those whose evenings were still free there was now a rival attraction. A Bingo Hall had opened where Beeston Essoldo once stood, and many of the women and their menfolk preferred to spend their evenings there. Only a few could play darts, it was said, but anyone could play bingo. Besides, bingo kept you from beer, and there was always the chance of winning, which meant putting money in pockets that were becoming emptier.

And for those of all ages with pockets reasonably full still, and who didn't fancy stuffing themselves with beefburgers or chicken and chips, you could now nip into Nottingham, where both the Alfreton and Mansfield Roads boasted growing numbers of Chinese, Italian and Indian Restaurants. And if you preferred to stick with English food, then try the Berni steak houses, of which there were several. An increasing number in work were becoming car owners, even if they were second-hand cheapos; parking on most roads in the city was free, and before you sat down to eat you could always have a snifter in one of Nottingham's more glamorous public houses.

Even Arthur, the staunchest of Beeston loyalists, reported back one Saturday that the previous evening he'd gone into the city and stood in Yates's Wine Lodge for a good hour, drinking while he looked about him. 'Bleddy 'ell,' he said, 'full of tarts it was, all on 'em at the Australian port. And a bleddy trio in the gallery, pianner and what not, scrapin' out music like you've never heard. It were Skeggy and the Albert 'all in one.'

Dazed by the experience, Arthur vowed he'd never return, that was for sure.

'Didn't you fancy a chicken vindaloo, then?' he was asked.

'What's that when it's at 'ome,' Arthur asked. 'Bleddy foreign muck? I'd rather chew rusty razor blades.'

It would be more than a decade later before Beeston began to acquire what a friend of mine called 'night-time exotica'; in the late nineteen-seventies the town's three fish-and-chip shops still exhausted the evening's possibilities for those who had no liking for what 'Mac's' and KFC could provide.

***

The three-day week had been and gone, but it, too, changed habits. More of the older drinkers, men as well as women, stayed in at night. And some of the locals who called in at the Oak came with jugs, and when these were filled with beer they headed home for an evening in front of the tele. Some twenty years before there had, I recalled, been dire predictions that with the arrival of TV, cinemas would empty and other forms of evening entertainment were bound to suffer, pubs included.

Yes and no. Beeston's High Street had at one time included no fewer than three cinemas. The first, Kozy Drome, dated from nineteen-thirteen. (Motto: 'Go in laughing, come out scratching.') I was told this by a banjoist I played with for some years, John Bly, whose uncle had been the projectionist there. The last of the three, called, I think, the Palace, closed its doors not long before we arrived in the town. But two Essoldos on opposite edges of Beeston still hung on, although they, too, would soon disappear, one to become the aforementioned bingo hall (now a Co-op), the other a skating rink before being turned into a large petrol station.

As for Nottingham, in the mid-sixties the city had thirty-nine cinemas, and though many of these went dark in the following decade, sufficient remained for the clientele which chose to free itself from the stay-at-home drug of TV to be well catered for. And as there were plenty of bus services all around the city, living in the wastes of Beeston was no bar to attendance at one or other of Nottingham's 'flicks'.

Nor, from all I was told, did pub life greatly suffer from the coming of the 'box in the corner'. It was more the increase in unemployment. It was then that 'family entertainment' in front of the tele gained in popularity, for a while at least. But local pubs, including the Oak, held firm. The pub might not offer a great deal by way of formal entertainment, but, as this narrative has frequently suggested, it was a place with a sense of community. It had to be, because those who drank there were almost without exception locals, a mixture of factory and office workers, some tradesmen, a few connected in various ways to the local university, and a scattering of others – Harold, Ian, others including some (very) small time criminals, all of whom enjoyed a drink and conversation ….

I don't want to sentimentalise this. In the days before I knew it, the Oak must have had its prejudices, though as far as I could tell they didn't include race or sex. For a while one of the regulars, a fitter at Ariel Pressings, was a black Jamaican, called Huey. Huey was, Sub Sid told me, a good man with a fishing rod – they'd often go off together on Sunday mornings, fishing along the Beeston cut, or at the gravel pits – and I knew him as a jovial raconteur, who, on his evenings in the pub, stood in the passage beside Sub Sid and was always prompt to pay when his round came up. When he suddenly left, to be seen no more, it was because he'd been threatened by the husband of a woman he regularly went back to after an evening's drinking. She was a secretary at the Pressings who'd apparently neglected to mention the fact that she was married to a night watchman. The night watchman came home early one morning and Huey was forced to depart in less than dignified fashion.

As to the widely accepted notion that pubs were male-only strongholds, that certainly wasn't the case at the Oak. Leave the Ladies Darts Team out of it. There were the Saturday night card schools, there were the wives who regularly came in of an evening with or without their partners and who sat in the Lounge for an hour or two, and there were those, in Edie's time especially, who arrived, usually with a woman friend, for lunch, though one or two were on their own. I can't imagine anyone feeling out of place in the Oak. All could come in, 'the farmer and the clown'. It was a good venue to meet in, to fold your knees and have out your chat. Pauline quite often came with me, the wives and partners of male friends came, so did a couple of gay friends who made no effort to disguise the nature of their relationship.

But the Oak was changing, no doubt about it. Ian was dead, and we heard that Dennis and Doreen, who were missing for some weeks, had been required by their landlord to leave their flat. They owed something like six months back rent, and had shown no sign of being able to pay. So they had to go.

***

One day, when I'd dropped in to see Bill Cole at his house about a forthcoming gig – taking our lives in our hands by venturing north of the river, as Bill put it – he suggested we go across the road to have a pint at the Queen's. 'A chance for you to say hello to Derek and Edie,' he said.

But it wasn't an especially comfortable occasion. They both announced that they were pleased to see me: 'after all this time,' Derek said, insisting on giving me my pint 'on the house.'

'How's it going?' I asked, 'Business looking good.'

There was a slight but unmistakable pause before Edie said, 'Well enough.'

'Lunchtimes going strong? Feeding the hungry masses?'

Derek ignored the false joviality of my question.

'Not worth it,' he said, 'Not now Beeston Boilers have gone.'

I'd heard about the entirely unexpected closure of what had seemed a thriving concern, but I hadn't realised – or hadn't allowed myself to consider – the effect that was bound to have on the Queen's trade. Ought I to tell them what I knew? No, I thought, better to keep it to myself.

But years later I put something of what led to the factory's sudden failure into my second novel, *The Plotting*. The story as I heard it came from a friend, Mervyn Gould, theatre manager at Loughborough University where I was by then head of the English department. Before coming to Loughborough, Mervyn had been a lighting man and front-of-house manager in professional theatre, although when on one occasion work dried up he filled in as chauffeur to a couple of well-known London comedians. One day they had him drive them up to a small town in Nottinghamshire he'd never heard of. And as he navigated the Bentley up the M1, one of them gave him what he suspected was a heavily edited account of why they were making the journey. A solicitor they employed to look after their business portfolio – Mervyn spoke the word with a heavily ironic inflection – had told them of a business going at knock-down price. Eighty-four thousand in cash and no questions asked.

By midday they arrived at their destination – Beeston Boilers – and according to Mervyn half an hour later all was done and dusted and they were on their way back to London, the comedians poorer by eighty-four thousand smackers but now the owner of a factory, which, so he was later told, they sold to a property developer for a cool quarter of a million. A nice little earner, one of them said. And for a hundred or so loyal employees who had done no wrong, an end to their work. Dismissed with minimum legal notice. Thank you and good night.

Could I reveal any of this to Derek and Edie? No, of course not. They were hardly likely to feel better because of anything I could tell them about the rotten business. But what had happened meant that the move from the Oak was far from the success they'd hoped for. They would survive well enough, no doubt about that. They were a resourceful couple and, through Bill were soon able to organize jazz evenings which brought in a regular clientele. Good. And good that a newly established shopping parade diagonally opposite began to provide Edie with the chance to set up her lunchtime 'specials'. But this was largely passing trade. I heard later that Derek had abandoned his yellow sweater for shirt with tie and, in the evenings, regularly appeared in a maroon corduroy jacket. I suppose he was wanting to create a different image. No longer landlord of a small back-street pub but 'mine host' of a rather more respectable hostelry, one that, as my mother might have said, rather 'put on airs'. Would Harold have felt at ease in the Queen's? Would Arthur Crouch? Would any of the Oak's regulars? Some, no doubt. But by no means all. 'All come in, the farmer and the clown?' Not, I thought, to the Queen's. But to the Oak, yes. For the moment, at least, the Oak remained the small good place.

3: The Pub and Politics

Public House. Inn. Tavern. Places of hospitality, of food and drink, of conversation, of musical entertainment (sometimes) and fellowship. An image of sociality, of order in variety. And, through history, a place where political matters are either discussed or bring together groups of like-minded men (and, more rarely, women). A meeting place. A microcosm of society at large. Public Bar, Lounge, Snug …. Predominantly, however, a place for the commons rather than the nobility. Pubs may be named for Dukes and Earls and Kings and Queens, but you wouldn't expect to find a member of the nobility propping up the bar.

There were, of course, exceptions, in fiction at all events. Prince Hal consorted with Falstaff's merry crew at the Boar's Head, although the moment he became king he dropped the connection. 'I know thee not, old man.' A terrific moment in *Henry IV Part Two* dramatises the gap between Public and Nobility. Hastings, one of the plotters against Henry, himself gees up the other rebel lords at their meeting in the north country by telling them that what they plan is necessary. England expects. 'We are time's subjects, and time bids be gone.' The next scene is set in Eastcheap, 'Near the Boar's Head Tavern'. Here are the hoi polloi, the common people who will presumably be keen to see the king overthrown and a new order established.

Not a bit of it. They have their own troubles to worry about. Mistress Quickly wants to set the law on Falstaff, who has tricked her out of money. Others want a drink. What has any of this to do with setting the realm to rights?

Getting on for two and a half centuries later, Dickens in *Barnaby Rudge* makes the *Maypole Inn* into an image of Merry England, in the autumn of life but still ruddy with health and purpose. According to Larwood and Hotten, in their monograph

126

on *English Inn Signs* (1951) the pub Dickens has in mind was on the edge of Hainault Forest, and a sign on the stable door warns against smoking inside, which seems reasonable. Of other prohibitions we hear nothing. But other village pubs, under the influence of the clergy, were opposed to anything to do with maypoles because of their connection with sexual licence. During the Commonwealth period the object itself was banished from village greens, as were the dances that went with and around it, a decision Dickens would have loathed. And he equally loathed the fact that the Evangelicals of his day had succeeded in taking all enjoyment out of the one day of the week during which working people were free from their labours. His essay, 'Sunday Under Three Heads' is a scalding attack on those who legislate to ensure that joylessness be visited on working people, even while they themselves escape the rules they have created. And when at the beginning of *Little Dorrit* Arthur Clennam returns to London to see his widowed mother, he walks through Sunday streets where 'maddening church bells of all degrees of dissonance, sharp and flat, cracked and clear, fast and slow, made the brick and mortar echoes hideous…. In every thoroughfare, up almost every alley, and down almost every turning, some doleful bell was throbbing, jerking, tolling, as if the plague was in the city and the dead-carts were going round.'

These words were written in the eighteen-fifties. A hundred years later, when I was growing up in one of London's outer suburbs, and read Dickens's account of how, on an English Sunday, 'there was nothing for the spent toiler to do, but to compare the monotony of his seventh day with the monotony of his six days, and make the best of it,' I could at least rejoice that there was only one day of the week which enforced such monotony. But still on Sundays there were rules aplenty intended to put a block on people's pleasures. Many parks were locked, theatre and cinemas – not all – shut, opening hours for pubs were restricted, and most restaurants were closed all day. Peter Cook imagines a Corinthian family sitting down to breakfast when a letter from St Paul drops through the letter-box. 'Dear Corinthians,' it says, 'stop enjoying yourselves.'

When I began to make the Oak my favoured home from home, the regulars managed to enjoy themselves on Sundays though I can't believe they wouldn't have preferred to have done without Sunday Licensing Laws which restricted pub opening hours to a minimum. Even Bob found himself in agreement with Harold's occasional observation that 'it's one rule for the rich, another for the poor.'

***

Because the Oak was such a small pub it had no special meeting room of a kind that other pubs in the town provided for groups which paid for the privilege of their 'evenings'. Most of these were purely social occasions, dances, amateur theatricals, variety shows of the kind which put money in the pocket of the young Peter Christmas, though there were, of course, a number of clubs whose members came together on a regular weekly or monthly basis. The Pigeon-Fanciers, the Chess Society, the Philatelists, odd play-reading groups, and so on. There were also pubs whose meeting rooms played host to political organizations. Beeston's Labour group, having given up their lease on the shop premises which had been theirs for some years, now began to hold monthly meetings at the Station pub. This was a large, gaunt, red-brick building hard by Beeston Station, which had been built at the end of the nineteenth century, presumably in the mistaken belief that commercial travellers into and out of Nottingham would find it a preferable alternative to any of Nottingham's city pubs. It had an upstairs 'Dining Room', as well as several ground floor bars, and was more or less bereft of custom by the time we took to hiring the dining room for Labour Party meetings. There were rumours that if you shifted any of the old horse-hair settles in the Saloon Bar you'd probably find the bodies of dead drinkers from a former age which had lain there, undisturbed, for decades. It was that kind of place. But it suited our purpose, as it did the local CND group. (Which rejoiced under the acronym of BANG – Beeston, anti-nuclear group.)

At one of our party meetings a man in a camel-hair coat, with brown trilby and shiny new briefcase clambered up the stairs to where some twenty or so of us were gathered and asked if, as prospective Liberal candidate for the constituency, he could sit in on our debate. 'Of course,' we said. Someone, having suggested that there was no evidence whatsoever of a Liberal Party organization in Beeston, asked whether the briefcase might perhaps contain a tape recorder, and another wondered whether his coat had been loaned from the props cupboard at MI5. Much laughter, at which point he upped and left. There was general agreement that he hadn't been forced out by the taste of Ind Coope bitter, dubious though that was.

Meanwhile, The White Lion was becoming a meeting place for the National Front. (Did they choose the pub because of its name, I wondered: keep Britain white. Keep the Lion pure.) Spies reported that the group, most of whose members arrived by motor bike dressed in black leather, never amounted to more than a dozen, and I think that after a few months of handing out leaflets along the High Street, they gave up hope of recruiting Beestonians to their cause.

But a couple of years later they were back, this time with a cause to uphold. By nineteen eighty-two Beeston, along with many towns in the Midlands and North, was experiencing higher than usual levels of unemployment. I don't need here to rehearse the reasons for so many men being out of work, nor say much about the extraordinary unpopularity of Thatcher, the real loathing with which you'd hear her name uttered in the pub. The Oak had its share of working-class Tories, but at this time they kept their heads well down. *Labour Isn't Working*. That poster, credited with doing much to bring Thatcher her victory, was now the object of revilement. Thatcher really was *hated*. But then it all changed.

What brought about this change was of course the Falklands war. The Sunday after war was declared and the ships set out from Portsmouth, I was as usual having a lunchtime drink with a few friends, when a young man came into the Saloon Bar. He was wearing a Union Jack vest, torn jeans, and he carried a bucket which he shook in our faces.

'Support our lads,' he shouted. I recognised him. He was a winch-winder who lived on the local council estate, was often in the Public Bar of an evening, and had recently lost his work when the mine that employed him was mothballed.

We declined to put money in his pail, and he squared up to us. 'Ain't you patriots, then? Want the Argies treadin' all over us, do you?' He was heavily muscled and there was no mistaking the intensity of his words, nor his real aggression.

John, that naval man, came out from behind the bar. I've forgotten his actual words, but what they amounted to was that he himself had been in the navy, that he wanted no trouble, and that he'd rather keep the peace than have to call on the police to do it for him.

The youth shouldered his way through the drinkers, slammed out of the street door, and we could hear him shouting about the pub being full of commie bastards trying to do England down.

It was shocking, not merely in its unexpectedness but the absurdity of his claim. As someone noted, it was somehow typical that patriotism was not a British but, by implication, an exclusively *English* matter. And how extraordinary, that a man who only a few days previously had been cursing Thatcherism should now be vowing support for the Prime Minister he'd identified as responsible for his fate. We'd seen him on a march a week earlier chanting, 'Maggie, Maggie, Maggie, Out, Out, Out.' Now, as he disappeared along Villa Street, we could hear him bellowing 'Money for Maggie's Boys.'

But that incident in the Oak was by no means unusual. My son recently told me that he and some friends were drinking in a pub on the far side of Nottingham when a man dressed as a John Bull patriot came to where they were sitting, rattled a bucket in their faces and, when they shook their heads, threatened them with physical violence.

And meanwhile a straggle of National Fronters rode back into Beeston and once more began to hold meetings at the White Lion.

It was a strange time.

***

A few months later, after the war was over, Eric Hobsbawm published an essay in the journal, *New Society*, in which he argued that anyone bewildered by the amount of working-class support there was for Thatcher at the moment of the war simply didn't understand the degree of patriotism among the working class. As evidence of this he cited the readiness of workers to drink in pubs named for Royalty, for Admirals and Generals, and for the nobility in general.

This seemed to me a daft argument. I doubt many drinkers would make a name check before deciding whether the pub they were about to enter deserved their patronage. Besides, as I pointed out to my daughter when that autumn I drove her back to Norwich where she was a student at UEA, pubs were licensed by magistrates. Imagine the magistrate who'd be keen to hand a licence to a publican proposing to call his premises The Tolpuddle Martyrs, or The Peterloo Martyrs, or – I noticed from a road sign we were about to enter Thetford – or, even worse, The Tom Paine.

She pointed across the road. 'We're just passing a pub with that name,' she said.

I was so taken aback I insisted we drop in there for a drink. The place proved to be a modern roadhouse, all fake leather and oak beams, and as far as I could see the exclusive preserve of the gin-and-tonic set. Still, it made my point for me. I don't suppose any of the drinkers there knew or cared who Tom Paine was. A pop singer? A footballer? Just so, you could drink in a pub called the Royal Oak without being a monarchist, let alone knowing of what some historians chose to call 'the miracle of Boscobel'. In the middle of nineteenth century London there were at least twenty-six pubs bearing that name scattered about the city, and I'm damned if I believe that all their regulars were keen supporters of the monarchy.

Nevertheless, Hobsbawm was also right. The Falklands War changed Thatcher from Demon to Angel in the eyes of many working class people. It did so, I'm pretty sure, because the war gave them back a sense of identity, a feeling that they had a cause. It may also have signalled the possibility that once again Britain – for which read England – would be 'great' and that this would ensure their own emergence from the slough of despond into which the loss of work had cast them. In this sense Brexit echoes the Falklands war. Britain taking on the world, alone and indomitable.

Oh, the ironies of history. Because Reagan refused to help Thatcher in her battle against the 'Argies', she had to call on the dictator and murderer Pinochet to provide air strips for the re-fuelling of RAF planes taking part in the war. As a result, the dictator and murderer Galtieri would go down to defeat, the Islands – of which very few had heard and fewer still could point to on a map – would be saved for and by British forces. If this was what Hegel meant by the secret cunning of history in action, what it demonstrated above all was that such cunning makes a mockery of pure causes.

I don't suggest that these ironies were much discussed in the Oak, but the war, while it lasted, undoubtedly had its effect on pub conversations. One of my friends reported that his son's girlfriend worked as a librarian in the House of Commons Library. Following Michael Foot's demand that Thatcher should speak for England, the library was apparently crowded with MPs consulting atlases so that they could find out where the Falkland Islands actually were. Did one MP really believe they were somewhere off the north-west coast of Scotland? Arthur Crouch knew better. They were 'a bleddy long way off,' he said, and as far as he was concerned it would be better to 'leave the boggers alone.'

4: The Rising Star

The war was soon over, the bad feeling that had momentarily tainted the pub's air dwindled to a mere nothing, as though swabbed away by John's vigorous use of the mop, his daily doses of disinfectant as some of us called them. But something had changed. Nothing happened and yet much did. There were no blow-ups, no spectacular fallings out; but the Oak wasn't the same place. Regulars who while the war lasted had taken their custom elsewhere didn't return. You'd see someone you knew as a one-time habitué of the Oak coming along the High Street, raise an arm in salutation, and they'd cross the road, pretend not to have seen you, or suddenly find something to stare at in shop windows and keep their backs turned as you passed.

It wasn't absolute, this change. At weekends, especially Saturday nights, the pub would still be full. Cards, talk, games of dominoes, even an early evening use of the darts board. Bob still sat in his corner, Arthur would be in attendance, and Harold might show up for a pint before heading for The Commercial, which he admitted he now more often used. 'Admitted' was the word. There was an almost apologetic air to his revelation that he quite liked the atmosphere of the bigger pub, the fact, so he put it, that you could more easily get a seat in the Saloon Bar – Harold! who always stood in the passage at the Oak. And yet on the whole, Saturday nights were still beery, cheery, and if there were unfamiliar faces along the passage and in both bars, they quickly adapted to the pub's atmosphere.

But several erstwhile regulars, while they eschewed The Commercial, took to drinking in The Cricketers. Others became habitués of The Star, which was next to The White Lion, though possessed of a very different clientele. No National Fronters, though anyway with the Falklands war at an end these had once more vanished. I myself began to drop into The Star for an occasional evening drink. It was, after all, a Shippo's pub, so I told myself. Moreover, each of its rooms had considerably more space than the Oak. It also, so rumour had it, ran to basic lunchtime fare of the kind Edie had so spectacularly served up.

And then there was the entry hall. Roomily square, it could easily accommodate the company of men – never women – who stood there in order to drink a pint on their way home from work. Some of these came from the station, brought back by train to Beeston from their days in Nottingham, or Derby, or Leicester. 'International traffic,' someone called these men who wore office suits and sometimes carried briefcases. Among them was a man who answered to the name of Mick, grey-suited, with a David Niven moustache and a myriad of stories. Mick worked at Derby's Rolls Royce headquarters – I think as some kind of clerk – and as a non-car driver took a bus to and from work. It would have been quicker to go by train but Mick claimed the view from the bus window was far more attractive. The train went via Attenborough, Long Eaton, Spondon. No thank you. That name was enough to put you off your food.

Mick claimed to enjoy looking at the scenery as his bus rolled along the A 52 from Beeston to Derby Bus Station, and fellow bus travellers made good companions. He especially rated those who joined the bus at Bardill's Corner (Bardill's was a garden centre): 'Never open their newspapers, keep talking all the way through, and what they don't know about what's going on isn't worth knowing.'

'Going on where?'

'Anywhere,' Mick said.

He was a formidable drinker, Mick – he could have put Dennis, or even Doreen, under the table – but always jovial; he had his regular corner in the hall, and for us truants from the Oak he proved a welcome alternative to Bob's morose grousings. I continued to visit the Oak for a Sunday lunchtime drink, when I made a point of exchanging a word or two with Bob, who filled me in on the latest defections. 'Harold? Not seen the bugger for a good few weeks. And that middle-aged Teddy Boy, he's slung his hook. Dunno where he drinks now, and don't care.' He'd mention other names to which I couldn't put a face and always ended the same way. 'The rate we're goin' it'll be down to me and the barman.' (Meaning John.)

Fortunately I didn't have to listen to much of this. Sunday lunchtimes were usually the occasion for visits from writer friends including the poet and exhibition designer, Arnold Rattenbury, who would stay with us while he was producing one of his ingenious shows for the annual Nottingham Festival. We'd sit in the bay window, talking, laughing, drinking, until my then small son, as his older version recently reminded me, would be sent to fetch us for dinner, an errand which required him to run round to the Oak and stand outside the pub rapping on the window glass until we heard him. Then we all hurried home.

***

Soon after I took up my post at Loughborough University I interviewed a woman who was applying for a place as a mature student in the department. She was intelligent, obviously highly-motivated, and I was pleased to be able to recommend her to the University. As she rose to leave the room, she said, 'I think you know my husband.'

'Really?'

It was only then I looked with any attention at her application form. Her address was a street in Beeston near to my own. Name? But no, I didn't recognise it. 'I decided to use my maiden name,' she said. 'My husband is Lloyd Fricker.'

Who? And then it came to me. He was the smart-arse lawyer figure who with other council employees regularly came for Edie's lunches at the Oak. I remembered his talk of how many women he'd laid or expected to lay in the current year, his know-all air, his voiced contempt for his immediate superiors.

'Oh, yes,' I said, 'I remember now.'

A week later, Sunday lunchtime, Fricker came into the Oak, where I'd not seen him for several years. 'I was hoping to see you,' he said. 'I gather you've offered my wife a place in your department. Take good care of her, won't you. She's got two young kids to look after.' And he left.

Not difficult to guess his meaning. Take care she doesn't get attracted to some other man while she's on your premises. She's a mother. And she's my wife, I'm not having her look at another man.

It was alright for him to put himself about, screwing as many women as he could, but in no circumstances would his wife be allowed to escape his iron grip.

Sometime in the following term she arrived one morning for a tutorial with a black eye. She had, of course, walked into a door. I wanted to say, 'Leave the bastard, take the kids with you and leave.' But a head of department can hardly say such things.

Still, I was delighted when shortly afterwards she asked if I would support her application for a transfer to Nottingham University. 'I've got my two children to look after,' she said, by way of apologetic explanation. 'Now that I'm on my own with them I need to be nearer home.'

'Of course, I'll be pleased to help,' I said. I would be sorry to lose her, she was a very bright student. But she deserved all the help she could get.

As for Fricker, I never saw him again.

***

In nineteen eighty-three I was invited to join a Monday night jazz band, The Six Hot Pieces of Ginger, which played at The Nurseryman, a road house down from Beeston on the main Nottingham to Derby Road. (Later re-named Brian Clough Way.) There, I made a number of discoveries. In the first place, Shipstone's was a far better brew than the bilge water The Nurseryman sold, supplied by the same brewery that served The Commercial. That beer, so our trombonist Jack Nutbrown said, was all 'Gas and Gators.'

'Gaiters?'

'Alligators,' Jack said. 'Straight out of the swamp.'

Second, I discovered that The Nurseryman was a new kind of public house which wasn't really a public house at all. Such places, known as roadhouses, were going up all around Nottingham, as they were elsewhere in England. They were invariably positioned at roundabouts or major road junctions, themselves mostly new, and their intention was – had to be – to encourage a sort of monoculture. Instead of a number of small rooms, each permitting the creation of its own style and form of entertainment – darts, cards, conversation, whatever – these places, which could be entered by a number of doors placed at strategic intervals, were all one, vast room, carpeted throughout, with a couple of steps leading to an upper level where tables were laid for semi-formal meals. As for the meals themselves, they were variations on steak and chips, or breaded plaice and chips, or gammon and chips, or chicken leg and chips. The 'condiments', stuffed into small white china bowls, came in paper sachets.

Leave the condiments out of it, and was this so very different from the meals Edie served? Of course it was. Edie prepared her own chips, and fried them over the stove. These were all factory chips, ready-made and requiring only to be re-heated. And where Edie went down to one of the local butcher's for her sausages, bacon, and eggs – she favoured Albert Marlowe's – The Nurseryman got its food stuffs straight from some back-of-the-freezer truck supplier, from where it went into the roadhouse freezer and from there into the micro-wave.

It was hideous, this new kind of industrial enterprise. And it went hand-in-hand with a new kind of hybrid drinking establishment: part pub, part restaurant, neither one thing nor the other, and entirely lacking in the atmosphere that made a pub like the Oak so cherishable.

Soulless, characterless, synthetic, pretentious, the only feature of The Nurseryman that reminded me of a proper pub was a middle-aged man who came in every Monday night, ostensibly to listen to the music, but in truth in search of conversation, of the badinage he could have expected to find in the Public Bar or passage, had only the roadhouse run to such a space, which instead it existed to obliterate. Unlike, therefore, Bob or Mick, holding court in their own corners, Dave of The Nurseryman had to make do with a space along the endless bar, though at least his constant presence made one particular spot, *faute de mieux,* his own. Leaning there in his baggy black suit, Dave was ready to talk to anyone within earshot, to offer his opinion on matters grave and gay, and to let us in the band know the kind of music he preferred. Dave, it turned out, went far enough back to be an admirer of Ivy Benson and her All-Girl Orchestra, which in his youth he had listened and danced to at Nottingham's Lyceum Ballroom. Could we play any of the numbers associated with her? Such as, we asked? Well, Dave remembered that she'd given particularly affecting accounts of 'In the Mood', and 'With a Song in my Heart'. Not really our kind of music, we said, but we'll give it a go.

Dave also rated Doris Day's singing. And it was true, in her early years she had sung with a number of good American bands. But Dave was keen on 'Secret Love'. No, we said, we can't do that. Meaning, we won't. And as to 'The Deadwood Stage', forget it. But we can probably busk our way through 'Love Me or Leave Me', and we'll give you Wingy Manone's 'Jumpy Nerves', which everyone knows is the original of 'In the Mood'.

We played them both and we made a friend for life. Though none of the other clientele gave so much as a flicker of applause or recognition, Dave was enraptured, especially as we announced that the two numbers were being played in response to a request from 'The Gallant Gentleman at the Bar, known to one and all as Dave.' From then on, we had to play the two numbers on each Monday night gig, and as reward Dave never failed to buy us a round of drinks. The spirit of pub life was not yet dead.

5: *Departing*

One of the lingering consequences of the Falklands war was that it licensed a new, unlovely bullishness. A propos of very little, you'd hear people in the pub saying 'Shows you can't push old England about,' or 'We can teach those bloody foreigners a lesson,' or 'Let the world know we can still hold our heads up,' and these remarks would be accompanied with a kind of self-satisfied bracing of the shoulders. Those who voiced these sentiments were rarely the old regulars, the ones I'd known since I started drinking at the Oak. Among these, very little was said about the war. It had been fought, Galtieri had been defeated. Time to move on. 'Maggie' might be the heroine of the shining hour, but the unemployment figures were sill increasing, and all around Beeston mines were closing or under sentence of death.

Bob surprised me by voicing doubts about the war. 'Long way off, those Falklands,' he said to anyone who'd listen, 'men getting killed and ships sunk. And for bloody what?'

The words were overheard by a thickset middle-aged man standing in his Sunday best at the bar. He was a miner who'd retired with a bad case of white finger, someone who'd only recently begun to use the pub. 'You're war shy, that's your trouble,' he called out to Bob.

'I did my bit in the last lot,' Bob said.

'And we looked after your women while you was away. Took good care of them.'

John, who had been listening, stiffened. 'Get out,' he said. And then, louder, 'O-U-T. Out.'

The ex-miner was taken aback, then truculent. 'What's it to you?'

John repeated his order.

The other man looked around for support, but there was none. He left, slamming the street door behind him.

Nobody said much, but I suspect that we were all impressed. John had upheld the honour of the Oak. Even Bob muttered his thanks.

But that intervention, though it made John a temporary hero, couldn't prevent the pub's growing loss of custom. There was no dramatic falling-off, but Sunday after Sunday you could sense a gradual thinning out of drinkers. Fewer of the old regulars, and not many younger people to compensate for their loss. Most of the men who had once arrived after a morning in the garden or allotment either stayed away or, one after another, began to use other locals. Or of course were too old to get out, or had died. There had been a time when you could almost guarantee that you'd be able to buy your week's supply of vegetables 'in season' from the Oak. You'd put in your order one Sunday and the next it would arrive and be transferred from the grower's bag to yours. Potatoes, peas, runner and broad beans, cauliflowers, marrows, carrots …. Allotment holders weren't supposed to use their strip of land for commercial purposes, which meant that they weren't to sell their produce, but of course they all did. It was part of the life of the pub, banter about the size of Ted's marrows, or Harold's turnips, or withering comments about someone else's failure to produce the beans. Some grew flowers, and bunches were offered for the missus or lady-love of one or other regular. 'Here y'are, Ron, these roses will see you right for a nice Sunday afternoon in bed.' But most of that had gone. If you wanted your veg straight from the allotment, your best bet was to drop in on The Cricketers, where Ted now drank. And of course you had to buy him a drink, and one drink led to another, and then there was no time to pay a visit to the Oak.

Are drinkers a fickle lot? I don't think so. It's more that for a variety of reasons, not all of them apparent, pubs rise and fall in popularity, and the Oak, for all the excellence of its beer, was losing out to other pubs. 'Summer by summer all stole away'. And winter by winter, too.

***

In nineteen eighty-four I accepted an invitation to spend a year in Greece as visiting professor at the University of Athens. That August, just before I left Beeston, I went into the Oak early one lunchtime for a farewell drink. 'I'll be sure to send you a card from Greece,' I promised John, who said, 'Make it one of the waterfront at Piraeus, will you?' It turned out that while in the navy he had spent some time on shore at Athens' port. 'You won't find any good beer in the bars,' he said, 'but there's music most nights, and wine, too. A bit of an odd taste by all accounts, but you get used to it.'

'Perhaps I should try introducing the natives to Shippos,' I said, as we shook hands. 'Or tell them about the Oak.'

'I wish somebody would,' John said.

Then he cheered up. 'Dawn will be sorry to have missed you. She'd have wanted to say goodbye.'

'She's not here then?'

'It's her morning for the hospital. They're trying a new treatment on her leg.'

I'd noticed that these days Dawn was less frequently helping in the bar, and that, even with the aid of the caliper, her movements were increasingly slow, laborious even. 'I'm very sorry about that,' I said. 'Give her my best wishes, please, and tell her I look forward to seeing her once I'm back home.'

And John said that of course he would.

I'd wanted to buy a round for Harold and some of the others, but it was still early and none of the regulars were in. I had to ask John if he'd pass on my best wishes to Harold when he next looked in, knowing that wouldn't be for some time, and again John said that he would.

Not very satisfactory, but it was the best I could manage.

Part Four: Norman

1: Going

In September, nineteen eighty-five, a few days after my return to England from a joyous year in Greece, I went round to the Oak to pay my respects to John and Dawn. I'd sent them a few cards from Greece, including one of the waterfront at Piraeus, on which I'd written 'Recognise this?' Now I had with me a bottle of ouzo. 'I'll miss Greek drink now I'm back,' I'd planned to say as I presented them with the bottle, 'though not half as much as I missed Shippos while I was in Athens.' I knew John didn't drink, but Dawn liked an occasional tipple, and anyway the very smell of ouzo, that sharp, heady, aniseed scent, would surely bring back to John memories of rembetika in the waterside bars of Piraeus.

But when I pulled open the street door, the man behind the bar counter watching my approach was someone I'd never seen before. A stand-in, perhaps, while the landlord and his wife were on holiday? But no.

'They've been gone since Easter,' this man told me when I asked after them.

'Gone?'

'Had to give up the pub business. It got too much for the wife. Doctor's orders.' He looked at me. 'Are you the bloke who's been sending those cards from Greece?'

I nodded, but I was thinking of John and Dawn. The news of their enforced departure saddened me. They'd been conscientious hosts, and I'd never come across anyone who spoke ill of them. If they were still in the area I ought to visit them, give them the bottle of ouzo.

I asked for a pint of mixed and while he was pulling it, the man behind the bar, Norman, so he told me his name was, filled me in on the little he knew about what had caused the former tenants to quit. Dawn had been told she needed to have her leg amputated at the knee and medical advice was that afterwards she'd be better off looking for sedentary work. 'Hopping around on one leg would be doing her no favours,' was how Norman put it. Fortunately, John had a brother 'somewhere down in Devon' who needed help with his haulage business. So John had gone to work with him, and Dawn, so Norman understood, would put in some hours each week managing the books.

I wondered whether Norman had a forwarding address for them, but he shook his head. Nor did he know the name or place of the brother's business. In the Barnstable area, he thought. 'The brewery will have a forwarding address for them. Try Head Office.'

I said I would. Taking a pull on my beer – excellent as usual, I wondered aloud whether Norman had been in the pub business all his life. Somehow he didn't fit the bill as a landlord. He was grey-haired, thin on top, wiry-looking, fit. But no, it wasn't that. I got the impression he wasn't much of a conversationalist. Nothing tangible, but there was more than a hint of reserve about him. Not one for small talk.

Norman himself came to my help. He'd recently retired from the police force, he said, and several mates of his had recommended taking up pub work. 'Keep off the booze,' he'd been advised, 'and you'll be alright.'

'Occupational hazard, apparently, being carried to your bed,' Norman said. 'But I don't drink anything stronger than lemonade, so no problems there.'

'Join the club,' I told him. 'None of the previous landlords I've known here has had a drink problem.'

Norman nodded. 'That's the way to do it. Besides' he said, 'I like to keep myself fit.' He paused, 'And I know a bit about how to keep order, so I shan't be needing to call the cops.'

I laughed obligingly, but couldn't resist adding, 'I've been coming here for over fifteen years, and I've never known of any bust-ups at the Oak. Not physical ones, anyway.'

I wondered whether to mention poor old Sheffield Tommy, but his murder had nothing to do with the pub. And then I thought of Speedy and Simon and others on the wrong side of the law who'd been regulars at the Oak. I doubted we'd be seeing them again, not while Norman was in charge.

As though echoing my thoughts, 'Seems quiet enough, this place,' Norman said. 'Oldsters mostly, keen on a chin-wag and a pint. I'm not expecting trouble.' He made the pub sound like a retirement home.

I took my pint through to the Lounge Bar. It was empty. The painting of the oak tree still stood on the inner wall, and all else seemed the same, apart from a small Hammond organ that was pushed up against the wall directly beneath the painting.

I sat there in silence and then, having replaced my empty glass on the bar counter, and before heading down the passage to the street door I put my head round the corner of the Public Bar. A few men sat at tables, mostly on their own. I nodded at those who looked up at me but I recognised only one and I didn't know him well enough to say more than good evening. He looked at me blankly as though I was speaking a foreign language.

As I said farewell to Norman, who was inspecting a stain in his dark blue pullover, I asked about the organ. 'New to the pub,' I said. 'Do you have musical evenings?'

'Tomorrow night,' Norman said, 'come along, and bring your friends, too.'

'What time do you start?' I asked, and he told me that the evening usually got going about seven-thirty.

'I'll be there,' I said. 'Maybe bring my wife.'

But Pauline was otherwise occupied, and so the following evening, a Thursday, I rounded up a couple of friends – Bill Cole was out on a gig – and we made sure to get to the Oak before eight o'clock, hoping that would be early enough for us to grab seats.

We needn't have bothered. One or two drinkers, Harold not among them, stood clutching their pints in the passage, but there was nobody in the Lounge. Nobody, that is, apart from a lantern-jawed man with a dejected expression, droopy-eyed like a dyspeptic bloodhound, his dark jacketed form slumped at the organ stool. The instrument's lid was up, but there was no further sign of life. The man's hand was closed round a near-empty pint of beer and he barely nodded when the four of us entered.

'Are you the evening's entertainment?' one of my friends asked. He meant it jovially but it sounded a bit abrupt, so I added, 'We're looking forward to hearing you play.'

The man looked at us as though suspecting us of satiric intent. He got slowly up from the organ stool, straightened – he was at least six feet tall – drained his glass, and without speaking went out to the bar. We looked askance at each other. Had we come to the right place? On the right evening?

After ten minutes or so the man returned, his glass once again full. Nobody had entered while he was away. Sighing heavily, he sat down, facing the organ.

'May as well play something,' he said staring up at the painting of the oak tree. He turned briefly to us where we sat. 'Fancy anything?'

'Anything you play will be alright by us,' I assured him. 'Will Bob be in, do you reckon?'

'Will anyone?' the musician asked. 'Anyway I don't know Bob from bloody Caesar, do I? Why not ask at the bar.'

At that point, Norman stuck his head round the corner. 'Everything alright?' he asked.

'Keen to hear some music,' one of us said, and I asked about Bob.

'Bob? You mean that big lump that sits in the corner drinking brown ale?'

I nodded, and Norman said, 'He'll not be in this evening. Let it be known he's not keen on music.' He paused, 'Not keen on anything, if you ask me, beyond making as much bloody mess with his fags as he can.'

Then, to the organist, 'OK maestro, take it away. Perhaps some more will look in later,'

But nobody did.

The maestro played for half-an-hour and then he stopped. When he did we all applauded.

'Thank you,' I said. 'That was good. Really good.'

He looked at me sceptically, 'Really?' he said.

'Really. I don't much like the Hammond,' I said, 'but your version of "Lullaby of Birdland", was something special.'

The others nodded. We were all impressed by his playing.

He allowed himself a brief smile. 'Malcolm's the name,' he said, 'Malcolm Phillips. Not much of a name for a jazzman, is it.'

'There's Sid,' a friend said. 'Sid Phillips.'

Malcolm nodded gloomily. 'I was once on the bill with George Shearing,' he said. 'Before he went to make his fortune in the States.' He reached for his beer. Loquacity was setting in. 'I was on piano with the house band when he came through with his group. Manchester, that was.' He emptied his glass. 'You a muso?' he asked me.

'Trumpet and cornet, but not in your class,' I said. 'Still, I keep my card. You never know.' I was joking.

There was a moment's silence, then I risked asking, 'No offence but I was wondering why you included 'Black and White Rag' in your programme. What's that about – something to suit all tastes? I mean, it's not in the same world as Shearing, is it?'

Malcolm allowed himself a laugh it would be an exaggeration to call wry. 'Winifred Attwell,' he said. 'I wrote that for her, straight up. Wrote quite a few other numbers, too. Paid for dinner, and a bit more beside.' He shook his head dolefully. 'I had an agent in those days.' A pause. 'All dried up now, though.'

And he went for another beer.

While he was gone I told the others about Winifred Attwell. A black South African pianist who'd come to England soon after the war and made a name for herself on radio and the variety halls. She was probably good,' I said, 'but I was young, hardly even a teenager when she had her moment of fame, so I don't really know.'

When Malcolm returned with his beer I asked him what he thought of Winifred Attwell. Could she really play?

'She was OK,' he said, jazzman's litotes for good, even very good. 'She knew her way round the keyboard.'

'What happened to her, I wonder?'

But Malcolm didn't know. 'She had her hour upon the stage,' he said, startling me with the quotation. 'There were quite a few of them at that time, piano acts. Semprini ….'

'Russ Conway,' I said. 'His career was wrecked, wasn't it? when he was found with a male ballet dancer in his car late one night.'

'Yeh,' Malcolm said, 'Bastard papers and' – lowering his voice – 'bastard cops.' He was silent for a moment. 'Always seems to be piano players. Tony Davis, Strayhorn…'

'Liberace?'

'God help us,' Malcolm said.

***

Walking away from the near-empty pub at the end of the evening, one of my friends, Tony, said, 'A bit lowering for someone with that much talent to be plonking away in the back room of a pub.'

'Jazzmen get used to it. Still, it's worrying that so few were in.'

'If you ask me,' Tony said, 'that pub won't last much longer. Not under present management, anyway.'

2: Once a Policeman

After that first encounter with Malcolm, I made a point of dropping into the Oak on Thursday evenings. I admired his playing and I enjoyed talking to him. There was rarely anyone in the Lounge, and he and I spent much of the time in conversation, though every so often he'd turn to the organ and work through a number or two. Hoagy Carmichael, Earl Hines, Fats Waller. 'Stardust', 'Rosetta', 'Ain't Misbehavin'', 'Sweet Sue', …. We'd discuss our favourite jazz pianists. He was in no doubt that Teddy Wilson was the greatest. 'The jazz Mozart', he called him. I mentioned that Wilson had sometimes been known as the jazz Marx and Malcolm nodded. 'Cost him some jobs, apparently. But hear what he does behind the Lady and you'd want to make him King over all.'

'They don't have kings in America,' I said.

'Yes, they do,' Malcolm said, 'King Oliver.'

So then we ran through the titles jazzmen gave themselves, their ironic comeback on their actual status. Count Basie, Sir Charles Thompson, Duke Ellington – 'Emperor of the Universe,' Malcolm said, and I agreed – 'Earl Fatha Hines, Baron Treadgold….'

Who?

'He used to be big in down-town Beeston,' Malcolm said. 'He led a group called Big Bob's Be-Bop Bees. Saturday nights at the British Legion. Huge write-ups in the Beeston Bugle, especially after they signed to Embassy Records.'

'Embassy Records? That was Woolworth's label, wasn't it? Cheap rip-offs of top groups.'

'The very same,' Malcolm said. 'Trois and his Banjoliers play the best of the Basie Big Band.'

He seemed keen on such alliteration, so I asked, 'Has Big Bob been in to hear you, then?'

'Not yet,' Malcolm said. 'But a man can dream.'

Well, it was fun while it lasted but that wasn't for long.

'Back on stand for positively the last time,' Malcolm greeted me a few Thursdays later. 'After tonight the lights will go out and the curtain will fall on your musical treat.'

'You mean Norman's letting you go?'

'Difficult to believe, I accept,' Malcolm said. 'I told him the crowd was bigger and better than usual for jazz. One loyal follower. What more can you expect?'

'So what will you do?'

'Retire to my cottage and consider the many offers that will doubtless come my way. I may take up the invitation to become resident organist at Bramcote crematorium. Pay's good, regular work, and there's a clause in the contract that guarantees nobody will be allowed to throw their crutch at you.'

'How can that be guaranteed?'

'Anyone carrying a crutch will be denied entry.'

'In that case you may find yourself playing to one only, like here.'

'Exactly,' Malcolm said, in his best, hangdog manner. 'Music to die for.'

One thing I've always loved about jazzmen and women is their wit: a kind of cultivated, unsmiling, down-at-heel irony.

I told Malcolm I was sorry he'd be leaving, adding, 'that's one less reason for coming to the Oak.'

'Don't be hard on Norman,' Malcolm said. 'Like the cinema pianist, he's doing his best.'

No doubt he was, but before Malcolm's departure, whenever I dropped in for an evening drink, the place was virtually empty. Even the weekend crowds were beginning to thin, and although the beer was still well kept the atmosphere was pretty sepulchral, more like a chapel of rest than a pub. At this rate, Malcolm could be re-hired.

Even Bob's visits were becoming irregular, though I learnt from Arthur Crouch, whom I met by chance in the High Street, that this was because years of heavy smoking had led to heart and lung problems. 'If you ask me,' Arthur said, 'he's not long for this world.'

'And you,' I asked him, 'are you keeping well?' Because it occurred to me I'd not seen him since my return from Greece.

Arthur laughed his wheezy laugh. 'I'll do,' he said, and went on his way. There had been no mention of perhaps seeing me in the pub.

***

A few days after that fortuitous meeting with Arthur Crouch I went round to the Oak for an evening drink with a friend who still taught at Nottingham. We took our beer into the Lounge, now bereft of Malcolm's organ, and as Peter looked around him he said, 'Well, at least we shouldn't have any difficulty in hearing each other speak.'

The only other occupants were a couple sitting in what I thought of as Bob's Corner. I recognised the man, short, fair-haired, with an expression on his clean-shaven face that seemed fixed there, a kind of glowering sneer that reminded me of how I always thought that Dickens's Bentley Drummle must have looked, though Drummle would have worn far more expensive and fashionable clothes than this man's old jacket and jeans, and anyway he wouldn't have been seen in a pub like the Oak. But then Drummle wouldn't have been seen in a place like Beeston. I'd seen this man, whose first name I suddenly remembered was Gerry, around the town with a succession of young women, most of them pretty in a washed-out way.

The one now sitting across from him was no exception. Long, blonde hair reaching to the shoulders of her pale raincoat, a roll-top green sweater, she was looking intently at him, and when she spoke her voice was scarcely more than a whisper – chiefly, I thought, of agreement with whatever he said.

I turned my attention to Peter. We were sitting in the bay window, facing each other at a small table, and Peter, his back to the other couple, was telling me of changes in the English department, who had left, which newcomers were proving good company, when something, I don't know what exactly, made me look past him to the other side of the room. Had the woman spoken more loudly? Her face was flushed, and she was staring at the man called Gerry, as though transfixed. As I looked he picked up his glass, banged it down on the table between them, the bottom of the glass broke away, and he reached across and, hand round the body of the glass, and with an almost casual movement jabbed it into the young woman's face. She screamed – no, sobbed – a red ring appearing round her right eye.

I shouted, stood up, but before I could move Norman was at their table, stick like an elongated cudgel in his hand.

'Get up,' he said. His voice was thick, he was quivering with rage.

Gerry looked at Norman. 'Why should I?' he said. But his look was uncertain.

'Get up,' Norman said again, and the menace in his words was unmistakable.

To the young woman, he said, 'The toilet's at the back love, wash your face, make sure no glass gets into your eye.'

By now Gerry was standing, backed up against the wall. 'You little shit,' Norman said, poking the heavy stick into the man's ribs. 'Stay where you are or I'll break your neck.'

As he spoke he backed out of the Lounge, said to me, 'Keep him there,' slammed the door shut and a moment later we heard him shouting into the pub's phone.

Then the Lounge door opened and he was back in again.

For several moments nobody spoke, after which the young woman returned, the circle round her eye weeping blood.

'Don't hurt him,' she said to Norman, 'he's not worth it.'

'He's costing me my reputation,' Norman said as we heard the wail of a police siren coming up Villa Street. 'And he's damaged you. You'll need to get to A&E, get that seen to.'

She looked confused but Norman said, 'Don't worry, love, an ambulance is on its way. They'll look after you.'

Later, as I explained to Peter all that had happened – because he was sitting with his back to the incident he had seen little of the action, and by the time he turned round Norman was already at the table where the couple sat – I realised how well the landlord had handled the moment. He was obviously holding himself back from whacking Gerry and at the same time doing the right thing in protecting the young woman who by now would be on her way to hospital, as her assailant would presumably be in police custody. And from there to court.

Though, 'Don't be so sure,' Norman said as he joined us for a moment. 'That sort have always got a way of wriggling out of it. They'll book him, maybe put him into the cell overnight, and first thing tomorrow he'll be off to find himself a smart lawyer.'

His words made me think of Lloyd Fricker, he'd be ideal for Gerry, but I'd heard that he had left the town.

'Well,' I said, 'I hope you won't mind if I say I was mighty impressed by the way you coped with that.'

'My training,' Norman said. 'I've had to look after nastier bits of work than him. But I don't want riff-raff like that in the Oak. It's hard enough to keep the place going, as it is.'

For a moment I thought of saying something stupid like, 'People will be crowding in to see the hero of the hour,' but I'm glad I kept my mouth shut. Norman could do without crass attempts at praise. It wasn't praise he needed, it was custom.

As we walked away, Peter said, 'Does the Oak often turn into a rough house?'

Perhaps he wasn't being serious, but as he spoke I realised that I'd never before seen or heard of any incident to equal that. The Oak may have been – no, was – a back-street pub, but in its halcyon days there'd never been a whisper of violence. The heavies kept away. For all the petty crims who from time to time made it their watering hole I'd never even thought of the Oak as a place that tolerated violence. The nearest we'd come to it was the evening of Sheffield Tommy's murder, and that event, ghastly as it was, had only the most tangential of connections with the pub. In my years of going there, I'd witnessed a few shouting matches but they had always ended with, at worst, some sulks or slammed door exits, nothing worse.

'Well,' I said, 'Gerry won't be showing his face again, not while Norman's the publican, anyway.'

'He could have scarred that poor woman for life. Let's hope he gets a custodial sentence.'

We stood at the bus-stop waiting for the double-decker that would take Peter back into the city. As he boarded the bus, he said, 'But he'll probably get her to appeal on his behalf.'

He was right. When some months later Gerry Mayfield's case came up at the Magistrate's Court he got off with a heavy fine on the proven charge of causing a disturbance of the peace. There was no mention of grievous bodily harm. The case merited a few lines on an inside page of the city's *News*. The accused was 'Of previously good conduct,' the court learned, and his partner, by now the mother of a baby daughter, had forgiven him. The Royal Oak was not mentioned by name, nor of course was Norman.

3: Future, What Future?

For several weeks after that evening I didn't go back to the Oak. I was busy finishing a book on modern English poetry I'd promised to deliver to my publishers by the end of autumn, and I hate missing deadlines. On the occasions I slipped out for a drink, I'd take myself to The Star. One way and another I didn't get to the Oak for well over a month, one month became two, then three ....

But I thought about the pub a good deal. The speed of Norman's reaction to Gerry's sickening treatment of his partner remained in my mind. He must have seen from his position behind the bar how the scene was shaping up, but even so it all happened in what to me seemed the blink of an eye. It came to me, then, that either he knew about Gerry, perhaps even recognised him from some earlier occasion, or could somehow smell the threat on him. Policeman's intuiton? I wondered whether he'd be called to give evidence at Gerry's trial, or would he want and be able to keep his name out of it? (As proved to be the case.) Norman didn't want the good name of his pub dirtied. That much was obvious. But also obvious was the fact that the Oak wasn't any longer a pub many people would choose to visit.

And then another thought came to me. A pub community is essentially a floating, ever-changing group of men and women, brought together for a while in the one place but bound by few ties, and really pretty well ignorant of each other's life-long habits or deeper ties and commitments. It was as though by mutual agreement we left a good deal of ourselves behind when we stepped through the pub's front door. Even out in the street we could be almost shy in each other's presence. *This* wasn't where we were supposed to meet. The passage, or the Public Bar, or the Saloon/Lounge – these were the places where we could be familiar with one another. You might take a friend to a pub, but you'd not make one by going there. Harold, Arthur, Ted, Ian (now dead) others … No, not really.

As I thought about this I realised that the Oak was no longer a place I wanted to spend time in. Besides, as the months went on, I grew to accept that if I dropped in at The Star I'd find someone to chat with, as was hardly the case nowadays at the Oak. Mick would almost certainly be in residence, and after all, the Shipstone's ales served at The Star were at least as good as those on tap at the Oak. Autumn turned to winter, my book was at the publishers, other writing summoned me to my desk, and so it went.

But then, one wintry evening rather more than a year after my return from Greece, curiosity drew me back to my once favourite pub. I was curious to see if after all this time any at all of the old faces were still there, or if, like me they'd chosen different places to drink, or had left the area, or, who knew, had died.

As I came up Villa Street, I noticed a new-looking Ford Mondeo standing outside the street door, and when I stepped into the passage I saw that the man behind the bar waiting to greet me was someone I knew, though not well. He was the husband of one of the long-disbanded Ladies Darts Team, someone I'd often sat beside on the coach bearing us to a pub where his wife would be performing.

'Helping Norman out,' he said, as he poured my pint of mixed. Len. The name came back to me.

'You must have done that before,' I said, admiring the expert way he handled the pumps. Nice and steady, filling my glass to the top but little for the slop tray.

'Years of practice,' he said. 'I used to look after the bar at the Legion Club.'

'But not now?' I said as I handed over my money.

'I still do an evening or two. Quite a few of the lads and lasses from here use the place, especially when there's a variety evening. We had that Gerry and the Pacemakers last Saturday. A full house, we had for them. They were alright, too. Nosmo King compèred.'

'I remember him from one or two jazz gigs,' I said, 'He'd act as MC at Miners' Welfare Do's. He must be pretty old by now.'

'His jokes are,' Len said.

As I looked around me I realised that the pub looked even emptier than I remembered. Voices came from the Lounge, but when I glanced in on the Public Bar I saw it was more or less empty, and the few drinkers sitting at separate tables had little to say to each other. The juke box was silent. 'As quiet as the proverbial grave,' I said.

Len put a finger to his lips. 'Careful,' he said, keeping his voice low. Then, speaking at normal volume, he said, 'You'll find Norman in the Lounge. With some gentlemen in suits.' And he winked.

There were two of them, plus Norman, crouched round a table, sheets of paper spread out between them. Norman nodded in friendly fashion when I greeted him, though he didn't introduce the men with him beyond saying, 'We're going over design plans.'

I took my drink over to what I always thought of as Bob's corner and sat listening.

They were discussing alterations to the pub's interior. At least the two men in suits were. Smart, dark grey three-button business suits, with equally smart business lingo. Norman, in his customary dark blue sweater and jeans, chin in hands, looked on as they used pencils to indicate areas of what were evidently architectural plans. And the plans were for ways of 'improving' the pub so as to 'enhance its viability' as a 'profitable business venture' in order to 'maximise its potential'. To hear them you'd have thought they were discussing Oxford Street.

After some further half an hour of this, the two suits folded up their tents, preparing to depart. That's to say, they pushed papers into their attaché cases, stood, shook hands with Norman, refused his offer of a drink, and left. Theirs had of course to be the Mondeo.

Norman gathered together his own notes, then came over and stood beside my table. I wondered whether he'd challenge me about my long absence, but no. 'Those gents are employed by the brewery,' he said, as though in self-defence. 'Design consultants.' It was as though he was saying, 'Nothing I can do about it.' Instead, he said, 'The brewery is planning to modernise quite a few of its properties, and we're one of those on the list.'

He looked evasive, almost embarrassed, and I didn't like to press him on what exactly had been going on. Anyway, it was obvious that what the Oak needed was not a face-lift, it was customers, and I was far from sure that making a few alterations to the pub's interior would bring drinkers clamouring for admission.

A few alterations, did I say? Not a bit of it. I was soon to discover that the alterations planned for the Oak were far more drastic than any I'd imagined, and they didn't improve the pub, they ruined it for once and all.

***

When I walked up Villa Street a couple of weeks after the design consultants had paid Norman their visit, a builder's lorry stood outside the pub, several white vans were parked alongside, and large, printed notices in the front windows of both Public Bar and Lounge announced **CLOSED FOR ALTERATIONS AND MODERNISATION.**

There was no mention of when next the pub would open. I paused, listened at the open door, heard sounds of banging, shouted orders, laughter, saw floating of dust in the passage, but I could make no sense of what might be going on inside.

Nobody, not even former regulars, showed much interest when I mentioned the Oak's changing fortunes in The Star. Indifference was nearer the mark. A shrug, a wry smile, a turning away, a few mild sarcasms, 'Take it down in easy stages, else it'll fall on yer'; 'Cart the bogger off to the knacker's yard'; 'Turn it into an old people's home, mi duck, that's the best thing for it' …. The Oak, it seemed, had had its day.

'You'll change your minds when you see the pub in its new glory,' I said. 'Not that you lot will be let in. Norman tells me that he'll be barring entry to the riff-raff. He's aiming at a classier clientele.'

'You mean Bob will have to put his teeth in,' someone said, and there was general laughter. But someone else said, 'Bob's not long for this world from all I hear,' and the subject was changed.

The pub stayed closed for over three months. Then word got around that there was to be a grand re-opening of The Royal Oak the following Wednesday. Rumours that the then current mayor of Beeston would be in attendance were widely disbelieved, though we learned that some of Shippo's top brass would turn up for the occasion. Drinks would be on the house.

I couldn't manage to get to the pub on opening night and it was Friday before I was able to stroll round to see what had become of the Oak. At seven o'clock that evening I walked up Villa Street, past the Snooker Hall and, further along, the new mini-parade of shops that now occupied the site where the lace factory had once stood.

The pub's woodwork had been newly painted and the street door was shiny black, an ornate brass knocker where the old, worn handle had for years done service. I faced the door, paused, drew breath, pulled open the door and stepped into the passage ….

But there *was* no passage. Nor was I standing on the old, cracked, red and black floor tiles I'd known for years. Instead my feet trod on brand-new parquet flooring.

And the passage walls had entirely vanished. There was therefore no Public Bar to the left, nor Lounge to the right. Instead the pub was one large undifferentiated space in which the bar had been pushed further to the rear and now took up the entire kitchen space where once Edie had cooked.

Three or four high steel stools with padded black seats fenced the bar off. As for the bar counter, it was broader than formerly, and the wooden front, with brass rail round its base, was surely fake.

Dazed, shocked even, I took a step or two forward, my footsteps clacking on the bare boards, and then I paused to look around.

The place was empty. Empty, that is, apart from one or two youths huddled round a fruit machine that stood against the wall which had once housed the Lounge's fireplace. High above the machine, pinned almost at ceiling height, was the painting of the oak tree that Edie had once, in a different age, bought for the pub. Out of sight, out of mind. Two formica-topped tables were jammed against the former Public Bar's bay window, but they did without chairs, and I realised that if you wanted to put down your glass you had to make use of one of the narrow shelves that surrounded the four columns – two each side of the door – which stretched up to the dark brown painted ceiling. The shelves were just below shoulder height, and above them were lengths of mirror, and above *them* small strip lights shaded by brass fittings set the mirrors aglitter with the reflected glare of the lit lamps. The whole place felt chill, stripped, barren.

I thought of Dickens – when *don't* I think of Dickens? – and his account of the sun over Marseilles and how its comfortless stare made the eyes ache. Comfortless, yes, that was it. That was what the Oak had become.

As my vision settled, I saw Norman. He was waiting behind the bar for my approach. No longer in his dark blue sweater, he was, under orders in all likelihood, wearing a cream jacket over white shirt and maroon tie.

He looked as awkward as I felt, though his greeting was friendly enough.

'Shame you weren't in on Wednesday,' he said. 'We had quite a full house.'

Without asking he poured me a pint of mixed, and while he did so I took in the cooler cabinet under the bar and the bottles it contained. Wines, chilled beers, small bottles of what were almost certainly ready-mixed cocktails.

'On the house,' he said, pushing the filled glass over to me. I took it, raised it, thanked him, and said, 'Well, here's to the new-look Oak.' I tasted the beer. Mercifully some things don't change.

'What do you reckon?'

'The beer?'

'The Oak.' Then, as though not wanting to hear what I might have to say, he said, 'It's a fresh start see. We've got to adapt to changed circumstances. We're looking to attract a younger clientele.'

We? Who did he think he was kidding?

I pretended to look round, appraising with due care and attention what had been done to the place.

Nowhere to sit, no chance of pub games, of darts, cards, dominoes.

'It's called a vertical drinking experience,' Norman said, and I couldn't tell whether he was being ironic. 'Clear the floor space and get more in. If people are standing they tend to drink more quickly.'

'Is that so?' I said.

And then what? More fights? I suppose I was thinking of Gerry Mayfield though I kept my thoughts to myself.

'Then most of them will want to go on to a restaurant. Or maybe a night club.'

'Last time I looked Beeston wasn't exactly full of night clubs.'

'They'll take taxis into town,' Norman said.

But he didn't believe it.

***

Not long afterward I was drinking with a friend in Loughborough, a man who had started his own micro-chain of pubs, when he told me that Shippo's directors had for some time been planning to sell the business to a far larger brewery, or was it a food chain? and that the original brewery, a handsome building on the far side of Nottingham, was to be mothballed and a preservation order placed on it. Well, good, at least the bastard developers couldn't get their hands on *that*. As for its pubs, there had, my informant told me, been the inevitable 'rationalisation' of premises, which of course meant that a number of Shipstone public houses were to be sold off and that the remaining ones had been taken under the new ownership, or closed down.

Including Beeston's Royal Oak?

No, he'd heard that the Oak was to be modernised.

'It already has been.'

'Oh, so that's where you drink?'

'Used to drink,' I said.

I never went back, and for years I even avoided walking up Villa Street. But then, a few years ago, I decided to cut up the Street on my way to a supermarket that stood directly behind the Oak and which, when it opened, had prompted a joke about the smallest pub in Beeston having the town's largest car park.

As I came near I saw that, outwardly at least, the Oak was unchanged. But the sign that had hung over the street door had gone and in its place a different board proclaimed that the name of the premises was now **Nimboo's** or something like it. I went across and standing on the wooden trap doors that led down to the cellars peered in at what had once been the bay window where I'd for so long sat with friends or on my own. Tables and heavy-duty chairs, white tablecloths, red-leather menus propped beside small unlit lamps.

The place had become an Indian restaurant.

Postscript.

It's now October, 2020, the year of Covid, and a walk up Villa Street reveals that the Indian restaurant's bay windows have been recently boarded up. Prior to the building's demolition, I shouldn't wonder.